# The Happiness Algorithm

## *How to Stop Chasing, Start Living, and Finally Take Control of Your Life*

**By Ken Konet, M.Ed., MBA**

# Copyright Page



For permission requests, please contact the publisher at:
www.Humbolton.com

This is a work of nonfiction. However, some names and identifying details have been changed to protect the privacy of individuals. The advice, strategies, and opinions in this book are based on research, real-life experiences, and the author's personal philosophy. They are not intended as a substitute for professional psychological, medical, financial, or legal advice. If you require specific assistance, please consult a qualified professional.

Cover Design by: Isabella Green
Interior Formatting by: Isabella Green

First Edition: 2025

ISBN: 978-1-966703-07-5

For bulk orders, special requests, or media inquiries, please contact www.Humbolton.com.

# Table of Contents

# How to Use This Book

**(Because we all need instructions)**

Alright, so you've cracked open this book. Step one: Congrats. Step two? NOW, actually finish it!

Because if you're like most people, you've got a stack of half-read books sitting on your nightstand, whispering, *"Remember us? We had so much potential!"* Not this time. I designed this book on purpose to make sure you actually get through it. That's right, I outsmarted your short attention span.

---

Here's how.

Why This Book is Broken into Bite-Sized Chunks

Look, most people start a book with good intentions.

- *"This is going to change my life!"*
- *"I'm going to read this every night before bed!"*
- *"I'll definitely remember everything and totally apply it."*

Yeah. No. Most people read a few pages, get distracted by TikTok, and forget they have ever bought the book. So, to prevent you from drifting off into the abyss of unfinished books, I've structured the book in bite-sized chunks—so you can actually absorb and apply what you learn.

## Here's how it works:

### Part A: The Wake-Up Call

This is where I hit you with the truth bomb.

- This section exposes the real problem you're facing (because let's be honest, you're probably not as self-aware as you think).
- It'll break down why you keep getting in your own way, and why most people are stuck in the same miserable loop.
- Expect some sarcasm, some real talk, and a few moments of "Oh crap, he's talking about me."

If you read nothing else, at least read Part A.
(But don't be that person who only reads about the problem and never gets to the solution. I'm watching you.)

---

### Part B: The Fix

Okay, so you've been called out. Now what?

- Part B is where I hand you the tools to fix your broken thinking.
- We'll reframe how you see stress, happiness, failure, and all the other things you've been handling wrong.
- You'll get strategies, examples, and sometimes a slap in the face (metaphorically) to get you to stop making excuses.

This is where change *actually* happens.

If you only read Part A and skip this section, you're basically just diagnosing yourself and then refusing treatment.
Don't be that person.

---

**Part C: The Action Plan**

This is the part where I make sure you don't just nod along like, "Wow, great advice!" and then do absolutely nothing with it.

- Part C forces you to apply what you've learned—because reading without action is just entertainment.
- You'll get simple, direct challenges that will rewire your brain faster than bingeing self-help videos on YouTube.
- This is where the book stops being something you read and starts being something you live.

If you skip Part C, congratulations—you just wasted your time.
Because nothing changes until you take action.

---

**How to Actually Get the Most Out of This Book**

Alright, now that you know how this book is structured, let's talk about how to use it. Because let's be real—I know you.

You might be tempted to:
✓ Skim through quickly and call it "reading."

✓ Jump ahead to the parts that sound the easiest.

✓ Read without actually applying any of it.

Nope. Not happening.

Here's how you actually make this book work for you:

1. Read one full chapter (A, B, AND C) before moving on.

- No skipping ahead.
- No cherry-picking the fun parts.
- This book is a system, not a buffet.

**2. Do the challenges in Part C. (Yes, actually do them.)**

- Reading without action is like buying a gym membership and never going.
- You don't get results from owning the book—you get results from using what's inside.

3. Don't just read this book. Reread it. Use it. Live it.

- Happiness isn't a one-time decision. It's a daily practice.
- You might need to come back and reapply these ideas whenever life punches you in the face.
- That's normal. It means you're doing it right.

---

Final Warning: Don't Just Read—Do. You bought this book for a reason.

You wanted to:

✓ Stop stressing over stupid stuff.

✓ Rewire your brain for happiness.

✓ Actually enjoy life instead of just surviving it.

Well, guess what? That doesn't happen just by reading—it happens by DOING.

So don't be another person who:

- Reads self-help books like they're collecting Infinity Stones, but never applies them.
- Thinks "knowing" something is the same as actually changing.
- Reads one chapter, gets distracted, and forgets to finish.

No more waiting. No more excuses. You ready? Good. Let's do this together.

# Introduction

You've Been Lied To About Happiness (But Don't Worry, I'm Here to Fix That)

**Alright, let's get something straight right now:**

You've been completely misled about happiness. I don't mean in a *"Santa Claus isn't real"* kind of way (though if you're just now figuring that out, we have bigger problems). I mean... in a, "*society has been feeding you absolute baloney* about what makes life worth living" kind of way. Because somewhere along the way, you were taught that happiness is something you must chase.

- You'll be happy when you make more money.
- You'll be happy when you find your soulmate.
- You'll be happy when you finally get six-pack abs and a yacht and a life that looks Instagram-worthy.

And so, you work your ass off, you hustle, you check off all the boxes—
Only to realize... you're still not happy.

Weird, right? Well, that's because everything you've been told about happiness is a giant scam. And today? We're going to break you out of it.

## Why Most People Are Miserable (Even When They "Have It All")

Let's talk about the real reason so many people are stuck in the happiness hamster wheel. It's not because they don't have enough money, success, or material stuff. It's because they keep tying their happiness to things they can't control.

- They think happiness comes from achievements—until they realize achievements feel empty after five minutes.
- They think happiness comes from other people—until they realize people are unpredictable and mostly insane.
- They think happiness is about eliminating stress—until they realize stress is just part of life, and avoiding it makes them weak.

The problem isn't their circumstances. It's the way they think about happiness. And the truth?

Happiness isn't something you "find."
It's something you train.

## Why This Book is Different (And Why You Won't Want to Burn It Halfway Through)

Look, I know what you're thinking.
*"Oh great, another self-help book telling me to meditate, do yoga, and journal my feelings away."*

No. This isn't one of those books.

- I'm not here to feed you toxic positivity. (Yes, life sucks sometimes. We deal with it.)
- I'm not here to tell you to "just be grateful." (Like, cool advice, but how does that help when your life is on fire?)
- I'm not here to sell you some fake formula for eternal bliss. (Because happiness isn't about being in a constant state of euphoria, it's about knowing how to handle life without losing your mind.)

This book?
It's about real, practical, no-BS ways to stop letting life control your mood—and start controlling it yourself.

Because if you:

- **Struggle with stress, negativity, or overthinking?**
- **Find yourself constantly waiting for happiness to "happen"?**
- **Want to actually enjoy life instead of just surviving it?**

Then this book is for you. And unlike most self-help nonsense? You won't feel like you're being talked down to by a guru in linen pants.

---

**What You'll Learn (And Why It's Going to Change Your Life)**

By the time you're done with this book, you'll know:

- How to rewire your brain so happiness becomes automatic (instead of something you have to "try" for).
- How to stop letting stress, negativity, and other people's stupidity ruin your day.
- Why failure is actually the best thing that can happen to you (yes, really).
- How to master emotional control—so you stop reacting like an angry toddler every time life goes sideways.
- How to deal with difficult people without losing your sanity.
- How to make happiness last—so it's not just some fleeting thing that disappears the second life gets hard.

Basically? You're going to learn how to stop being a victim of your own mind—and start actually enjoying your life.

Because once you take control of how you think, react, and frame your experiences?
Life stops feeling like an uphill battle.

---

**Who This Book is NOT For (Aka The People Who Should Just Put It Down Now)**

Look, I don't want to waste your time.

**So let's be clear—this book is NOT for you if:**

- You want a quick fix instead of actually putting in the work.

- You'd rather complain about life than take responsibility for changing it.
- You're hoping for some magical three-step process to eternal happiness.

Because let's be honest—if happiness was that easy, everyone would already be happy. But if you're ready to stop making excuses, stop chasing happiness like an idiot, and actually start LIVING? Then keep reading. Because this is your wake-up call. And this time? You're not hitting snooze.

---

**Final Warning: This Book Will Change You (If You Let It)**

By the time you finish this book, you won't be the same person who started it.

- You'll stop overreacting to dumb sh*t.
- You'll stop getting stuck in negative thought loops.
- You'll start seeing problems as challenges instead of disasters.
- You'll start creating happiness instead of waiting for it.

And if you actually APPLY what you learn? Your entire life will feel different. But that's on you.

I can hand you the tools.
I can show you how to reframe your thinking.
I can even make you laugh along the way.

But I can't force you to use it. That? That's your choice. So, are you in? Good. Let's do this.

# Chapter 1: How I See the World Differently

**Part A: Welcome to my Madness**

Alright, let's get one thing straight before we dive into this: I am not one of those "just think positive and everything will be fine" people. You know, the kind who tell you to smile through your misery like some malfunctioning Stepford robot while your life collapses around you. No. I am not about toxic positivity, where we pretend everything is great when it clearly isn't. That's how people end up snapping and throwing a blender through their office window.

I am, however, a master of reframing. Not because I was born with some mystical enlightenment gene, but because life has roundhouse-kicked me in the face so many times that I had two choices: roll around in the dirt crying or learn how to make something useful out of the mess. I chose the latter, mostly because I don't enjoy the taste of dirt.

So, let's start here: Happiness is not about what happens to you. It's about what you do with it. That's it. That's the entire premise of this book in one sentence. But since you probably paid for more than just one sentence, I guess I should elaborate.

---

Let me tell you a little story.

**"At Least My House is being remodeled for free!"**

September 11, 2017. Hurricane Irma decides to roll through my neighborhood like it had a personal vendetta against my house. Wind howling, rain smashing against the windows like it was auditioning for a disaster movie, and then—BOOM—the neighbors tree smashed through the living room ceiling, water flooding in, everything we owned getting wrecked. $174,000 in damages. The kind of financial loss that would make most people curl into a ball and whisper "why me?" into the abyss.

Now, was this situation great? Absolutely not. Did it suck? 100%. But did I sit there sobbing over it like a lost puppy? No. Because at least now my house was about to get a full remodel—for free.

See what I did there? The magic words: "At least." Two simple words that can flip any situation on its head. Now, I know what you're thinking. "Oh, so you're just some enlightened monk who never feels bad about anything?" No, no, no. I get frustrated, I get annoyed, and I absolutely swear at inanimate objects when they fail me. But what I *don't* do is let a bad situation own me. Instead, I own it.

And if you think this is just some weird coping mechanism I developed because life refused to be kind to me, well—yeah, kind of. But also, it turns out that this is actually how the brain works best.

**Why Your Brain Sucks at Happiness (But We Can Fix It)**

Let's talk science for a second, because I know there's at least one skeptical reader out there who thinks I'm just pulling all this out of thin air. (Hi, skeptical reader. Hope you're having a miserable time being right.)

Your brain is a problem-solving machine, not a happiness generator. It's wired to look for danger, problems, and everything that could go wrong—a leftover survival mechanism from the days when we had to avoid saber-toothed tigers and questionable berries.

1. **You wake up late for work?** Your brain screams, "This is a disaster! You'll be fired, become homeless, and have to fight raccoons for food!"
2. **Your partner breaks up with you?** "Welp, that's it. Time to die alone."
3. **Your car won't start?** "Perfect. This is how I die of hypothermia in a parking lot."

This doom-spiral thinking is your brain doing its job badly. It's stuck on worst-case scenarios because that's what kept our ancestors alive. But here's the problem: You are not being chased by a lion. You are just late for work, you are just going through a breakup, your car just won't start.

This is why reframing is a superpower. Because while most people sit around obsessing over what's wrong, people like me ask, "Okay, what's still good?"

Your partner dumped you? At least now you're free to find someone who actually loves you back.
Your weekend plans got cancelled last minute? At least you just saved $100 and gained a rare night to recharge in your pajamas without feeling antisocial.

This is not delusion. This is mental aikido. Instead of letting bad situations flatten you, you use their momentum to flip them into something you can now work with.

And here's the best part: This is a skill. Which means you can learn it!

**Part B: The Fine Art of Not Losing Your Mind**

So now that we've established that your brain is a whiny little drama queen that sees every minor inconvenience as the end of the world, let's talk about how to fix it. Because here's the deal: If you don't train your mind to think differently, life will chew you up and spit you out like expired gum. Most people let their thoughts control them instead of the other way around. They wake up, something bad happens, and they just *let* it ruin their day. Like they have no say in the matter. Like their emotions are a remote-controlled car and the universe is some chaotic toddler pressing all the buttons.

But what if I told you that you don't have to react that way? What if you could build a mental firewall against all the nonsense life throws at you? You can. And it starts with choosing your response.

**The "At Least" Reflex: Rewiring Your Default Response**

Now, let's do a little mental experiment. Imagine your worst-case scenario. (Not, like, *super* worst-case—we don't need to go full apocalypse here. Just something annoying enough to make you want to punch a wall.)

Maybe you lost your job.
Maybe you broke your leg.

Maybe your cat just knocked your coffee all over your laptop, and now you have to write your term paper from your phone like some kind of caveman.

What's your first reaction? If you're like most people, it's probably some variation of:
"This is the worst thing ever. Why does this always happen to me? My life is ruined."

Now, let's try again with a simple shift. Find the "At Least."

Lost your job? At least you don't have to deal with that micromanaging boss anymore.
Broke your leg? At least now you finally have time to catch up on books, movies, or Netflix.
Laptop fried? At least now you have an excuse to upgrade.

This is what I call the "At Least" Reflex. It's an automatic way of turning your first reaction from catastrophe to opportunity. And the more you use it, the faster and more natural it becomes.

I didn't invent this, by the way. Your brain is already wired for this—it's just out of practice. Ever notice how time automatically reframes things for you?

- The breakup that felt soul-crushing in the moment? Five years later, you look back and say, "Wow, dodged a bullet there."
- The job you thought was your *dream job* but turned out to be a toxic dumpster fire? Now you laugh about it over drinks.

- The embarrassing thing you said in high school that kept you up at night for years? Yeah, nobody remembers it but you.

Time does this for us *eventually*, but why wait five years to see the upside when you can do it instantly? If you train yourself to apply the "At Least" Reflex in real-time, you cut out years of unnecessary suffering. Instead of marinating in misery, you start flipping the script on your own life.

**How I Accidentally Became Unbreakable**

Now, I didn't set out to be some Zen master of reframing. I wasn't born with magical positivity powers. No, I learned all this the hard way—through one brutal life lesson at a time.

Take August 2017, for example. My mom had a stroke. A thousand miles away. Meanwhile, my wife was having 30-40 seizures a day and needed me there. So, what do I do? Abandon my wife to be with my mom? Stay with my wife and leave my mom to deal with this alone? Neither option felt good.

**But here's what *did* happen:**
My sister, who had a strained relationship with our mom for years, stepped up. She took care of her. They reconnected.
By the time I was finally able to visit, my mom was in better spirits than she'd been in years. She and my sister had healed something that had been broken for decades.

And then, just a few weeks after mom's stroke, Hurricane Irma ripped through my home.
And then, my wife had brain tumor surgery.

And then, two weeks later, my wife felt better than she had in years.

It was chaos. It was awful. And yet—every single disaster had something good hidden in it.

This is why I don't lose my mind when life throws curveballs at me. Because I've seen it happen repeatedly, every setback has a hidden advantage. Now, that doesn't mean every situation *immediately* feels great. (I'm not some weird monk levitating above my problems.) But what I do know is that there is always an "At Least," even if I can't see it yet.

**WARNING:** Know When to Put This Tool Away Before we go further, let's be clear: The "At Least" Reflex is for *problems*, not *tragedies*.

If you spill coffee, say "At least I'm awake." If your car breaks down, say "At least I'm safe."

But if you lose someone you love? If your life falls apart? Do not dare say "At least." "At least" minimizes pain. That works for traffic. It does not work for grief.

For the heavy stuff—the life-altering, soul-shaking stuff—we don't use "At Least." We use something stronger. We'll cover that in Chapters 4 and 5. For now, let's practice on the small stuff.

**The Secret to Unshakable Happiness**

Most people think happiness is about having good things happen to them.
Nope. That's a trap.

Happiness isn't about what *happens* to you. It's about what you do with it.

Here's the cold, hard truth:

- Bad things will happen to you. (I know, shocking revelation.)
- You will lose people you love.
- You will have financial setbacks.
- You will have moments where everything feels like a disaster.

The difference between happy people and miserable people isn't what happens to them, it's how they respond.

- Some people have everything they could ever want and are still miserable.
- Some people go through unimaginable hardships and still find a way to be happy.

The secret? Reframing. I don't wait for life to make me happy. I make happiness out of life, no matter what it throws at me. And if you think that's impossible, just wait. By the end of this book, you'll be doing it too.

---

**Part C: What You Just Learned (And What Comes Next)**

Let me be real with you: what I just shared is the foundation of everything else in this book. The stories I told you—Hurricane Irma, my mom's stroke, my wife's seizures and surgery aren't just anecdotes. They're proof that this works. Every single disaster in my life has, in hindsight, led me somewhere better. And the reason I'm happy—genuinely, consistently happy—isn't because I have a perfect life. It's because I've trained my brain to find the advantage in every setback. That's philosophy. That's the "why."

But philosophy alone won't save you when life punches you in the face. You need tools. You need a system. You need to know exactly what to do when your brain starts spiraling into doom mode.

That's what's coming next. In Chapter 2, we're going to expose the specific traps your brain falls into—and why most people stay miserable even when they have everything. And in Chapter 3? That's where I hand you the complete toolkit. The Three Paths. The techniques. The training protocol that will make reframing automatic.

But for now, here's your first assignment:

For the next 24 hours, just notice. Notice when something annoying happens and your brain immediately jumps to the worst-case scenario.

Notice that first reaction—the panic, the frustration, the "why me?"

Don't try to fix it yet. Just observe. Because you can't change what you don't see. And once you start seeing it? That's when everything changes.

---

And that, my friend, is the first step to becoming untouchable.

**Congratulations.** You just learned the most powerful mindset shift on the planet. Use it well.

# Chapter 2: The Happiness Equation - Why Your Brain Is Wired to Make You Miserable (And What to Do About It)

I got a performance review once that was 95% positive. Nineteen out of twenty categories rated "exceeds expectations." Glowing comments from my supervisor. Praise for specific projects I'd completed. A raise. A bonus. Everything you'd want in a review.

And one category—ONE—rated "meets expectations" instead of "exceeds."

Guess which part I obsessed over for the next three weeks? Not the nineteen things I'd crushed. Not the raise or the bonus or the praise. Just that one "meets expectations" rating. I replayed it in my head. Analyzed what I could have done differently. Wondered if my boss secretly thought I was incompetent.

Izzy finally asked me why I was so stressed. When I told her, she looked at me like I'd lost my mind. "You got a raise and a bonus and you're upset because of ONE category?" And when she said it out loud, I realized how absurd it was. I had objective evidence that I was doing well. Nineteen out of twenty categories confirmed it. But my brain had decided that the one negative thing was the only thing that mattered.

That's not a character flaw. That's neuroscience. Your brain is literally wired to do this. And understanding why is the first step to stopping it.

* * *

## Why Your Brain Is a Threat-Detection Machine (Not a Happiness Generator)

Here's what nobody tells you about happiness:

Your brain wasn't designed to make you happy. It was designed to keep you alive.

And for most of human history, "staying alive" meant being paranoid.

Think about your ancestors 50,000 years ago. They lived in a world where everything was trying to kill them. Predators. Rival tribes. Poisonous plants. Infections from minor cuts. The environment itself.

So evolution did what evolution does: it optimized for survival. And the way it optimized your brain was to make it obsessively scan for threats.

Your ancestor who heard a rustling in the bushes and thought "probably nothing" got eaten by a tiger. Your ancestor who heard the same rustling and thought "OH SHIT DANGER" lived long enough to reproduce.

Do that for 50,000 years, and you get a brain that's phenomenally good at detecting problems and catastrophically bad at appreciating when things are okay.

This is called the negativity bias. And it's not a bug in your mental software—it's a feature. A survival feature that worked great when threats were physical and immediate.

But in modern life? It's a disaster.

Because the threats aren't tigers anymore. They're abstract. They're future-oriented. They're mostly imaginary. But your brain still treats them with the same urgency it would give to an actual predator trying to eat you.

That's why one negative comment on your work erases the memory of ten positive ones. That's why you replay embarrassing moments from five years ago at 2 AM. That's why you catastrophize about worst-case scenarios that will probably never happen.

Your brain is doing what it was designed to do: scan for threats, magnify problems, and keep you in a constant state of alertness.

It just doesn't realize the tiger is gone.

* * *

## The Actual Math Behind Why Negativity Wins

Psychologists have studied this negativity bias extensively. And the numbers are depressing.

Bad events have roughly five times the psychological impact of good events of the same magnitude.

Losing $100 feels way worse than finding $100 feels good. Getting criticized hurts way more than getting praised feels rewarding. One bad interaction in a day full of good ones will dominate your memory of that day.

This isn't because you're broken or pessimistic. This is how human brains work. All of them. Including mine, including yours, including the brain of that annoyingly positive person you know who claims to "just choose happiness." (They're either lying or on really good drugs.)

Your brain is also better at remembering negative experiences than positive ones. Painful memories stick. Pleasant memories fade. That embarrassing thing you said at a party seven years ago? Crystal clear. That compliment someone gave you last week? Already fuzzy.

And it gets worse: your brain is constantly running predictive simulations about the future. And because it's optimized for threat detection, those simulations skew negative. You don't daydream about all the ways tomorrow could go well. You catastrophize about all the ways it could go wrong.

This is why anxiety is the default setting for most people. Your brain is literally imagining disasters that haven't happened yet and treating them as if they're already happening.

So let's be clear about what you're up against:

Your brain magnifies negative events and minimizes positive ones. It remembers bad experiences better than good ones. It predicts negative futures more vividly than positive ones. And it does all of this automatically, below your conscious awareness, every single day.

This is the machinery you're working with. This is why happiness feels like such an uphill battle.

Because it is.

* * *

The Happiness Equation (Or: Why Trying Harder Doesn't Work)

So if your brain is wired for misery, how do you actually become happier?

Most people try to solve this with addition. They think: "If I'm not happy, I must not have enough good things. I need more success, more money, more relationships, more achievements, more stuff."

So they chase more. And they get more. And they're still not happy. Because the problem isn't what they have—it's how their brain is processing what they have.

Here's the actual happiness equation:

Happiness = Reality - Expectations + (Your Brain's Default Setting)

Let's break that down.

Reality is what's actually happening in your life right now. Your circumstances, your relationships, your health, your work, your situation.

Expectations are what you think should be happening. The life you thought you'd have by now. The outcomes you feel entitled to. The way people should behave.

When Reality exceeds Expectations, you feel good. When Reality falls short of Expectations, you feel bad. That's straightforward math.

But there's a third variable that most people ignore: Your Brain's Default Setting.

This is the negativity bias we just talked about. The automatic threat-scanning, problem-magnifying, worst-case-scenario-generating machinery that's running in the background of your consciousness all day, every day.

And here's the kicker: Your Brain's Default Setting has veto power over the entire equation.

You could have amazing Reality. You could have reasonable Expectations. But if your brain's default setting is "scan for threats and catastrophize about the future," you're still going to be miserable.

That's why some people with objectively difficult lives seem content while others with objectively great lives are perpetually unhappy. It's not about circumstances. It's about the default setting.

And that's what this book is actually about: changing the default setting.

* * *

## How to Actually Change Your Brain's Default Setting (The Non-Magic Version)

Okay, so your brain is wired for negativity. Can you fix it?

Sort of. Not completely, but enough to make a massive difference.

Here's what you need to understand: you can't eliminate the negativity bias. It's hardwired. It's been there for 50,000 years and it's not going anywhere.

But you can train your brain to balance it. You can deliberately build new neural pathways that counteract the automatic threat-scanning. You can make your default setting less negative.

It's called neuroplasticity. Your brain can rewire itself based on what you practice. And the key word there is practice.

If you practice catastrophizing, your brain gets better at catastrophizing. If you practice ruminating on negative experiences, your brain gets better at ruminating. If you practice scanning for threats, your brain becomes a more efficient threat-detection machine.

But the reverse is also true.

If you practice noticing what's working, your brain gets better at noticing what's working. If you practice reframing negative events, your brain gets better at reframing. If you practice redirecting attention away from imaginary threats, your brain becomes less reactive.

This isn't positive thinking. This isn't pretending problems don't exist. This is deliberate attention training.

Think of your brain like a search engine. Whatever you tell it to search for, it'll find. If you constantly tell it to search for problems, threats, and worst-case scenarios, that's what it'll return. If you train it to also search for solutions, opportunities, and what's actually okay right now, it'll return those too.

It won't eliminate the negativity bias. But it'll balance it. And that balance is what separates people who are chronically miserable from people who can actually enjoy their lives despite the inherent difficulty of being human.

* * *

## What This Means for the Rest of This Book

Every chapter that follows is teaching you a different practice for retraining your brain's default setting.

The Three Paths framework (Chapter 3) is about training your brain to default to reframing instead of reaction or resignation.

The Asset Audit (Chapter 4) is about training your brain to notice what you've gained instead of only what you've lost.

Turning loss into legacy (Chapter 5) is about training your brain to find meaning in grief instead of drowning in it.

Setting boundaries with toxic people (Chapters 6 and 7) is about training your brain to prioritize your wellbeing instead of defaulting to people-pleasing.

Reframing failure (Chapter 8) is about training your brain to see data instead of catastrophe.

Gratitude practice (Chapter 9) is about training your brain to notice what's working alongside what isn't.

Stoicism (Chapter 10) is about training your brain to focus on what you can control and accept what you can't.

Every single one of these practices is a counter to the negativity bias. Every single one is about deliberately rewiring your default setting from "everything is a threat" to "some things are threats, and some things are okay, and I can tell the difference."

None of them will make you permanently happy. That's not how brains work. But together, they'll make you less automatically miserable. And that's actually the best you can hope for.

So back to my performance review story.

After Izzy called out how absurd I was being, I did something different. I forced myself to list—out loud—the nineteen categories where I'd exceeded expectations. Made myself actually say them. Made myself notice that nineteen things had gone well.

Did my brain want to skip back to obsessing over the one negative thing? Absolutely. That's its default setting. But I didn't let it stay there.

That's not positive thinking. That's attention training. That's manually overriding a 50,000-year-old survival mechanism that no longer serves you.

And that's what the rest of this book is about.

Your brain is wired to make you miserable. Accept that. And then train it to do something different.

# Chapter 3 The Hidden Patterns: Why the Same Problems Keep Happening

I once watched a friend go through three divorces in ten years.

Same story every time. "She changed." "He wasn't who I thought he was." "We just grew apart."

But here's what I noticed: Every partner had the same complaints about him. "You never listen." "You're emotionally unavailable." "You care more about work than us."

Three different people. Same exact problems. And each time, he was genuinely shocked when they left.

That's not bad luck. That's a pattern.

And the most dangerous thing about patterns? They're invisible to the person living them.

* * *

Your Brain Loves Patterns (Even Bad Ones)

Here's something most self-help books won't tell you: your brain doesn't actually want you to be happy. It wants you to be safe.

And the brain's definition of "safe" is weird: it means "familiar." Even if familiar is toxic. Even if familiar is slowly killing you.

Your brain is literally wired to repeat patterns because patterns are predictable, and predictable means you won't get eaten by a tiger. Never mind that there are no tigers in your suburban neighborhood—your brain is still operating on 50,000-year-old software.

This is why people stay in jobs that make them miserable. Date the same type of person over and over. Make the same financial mistakes. Have the same fights with their parents every Thanksgiving.

It's not weakness. It's neuroscience.

But here's the good news: once you can see the pattern, you can break it. But you have to be willing to look at it honestly, which is harder than it sounds.

* * *

The Three Paths (And Why Most People Pick the Wrong One)

When something goes wrong in your life—and I mean really wrong, not "I stubbed my toe" wrong but "my entire plan just exploded" wrong—you basically have three options:

Path One: Reaction

This is the panic button. The fight-or-flight response. The immediate emotional explosion.

Someone cuts you off in traffic? You lay on the horn, flip them off, and spend the next twenty minutes imagining elaborate revenge scenarios.

Your boss criticizes your work? You either fire off a defensive email you'll regret later or spend the rest of the day stress-eating and catastrophizing about getting fired.

Your partner forgets your anniversary? You're either picking a fight or giving them the silent treatment for three days.

Reaction feels good in the moment because it releases all that pent-up energy. It's like popping a blister—immediate relief, but you've just made the wound worse.

The problem with Reaction is that it never actually solves anything. You're just vomiting your emotions onto whoever is nearest and calling it "being authentic." Spoiler alert: that's not authenticity. That's just being an emotional toddler.

Path Two: Resignation

This is where most people end up. It's the "I guess this is just my life now" path.

You hate your job, but you've got bills to pay and you're too old to start over anyway, right?

Your relationship is fine. Not great, not terrible. You're roommates who occasionally have sex and mostly ignore each other. But hey, at least you're not alone.

Your health is declining, but everyone gets older. Pass the fries.

Resignation is quiet suffering. It's the slow death of hope. It's when you stop believing things can get better, so you just... endure.

The worst part? Society rewards resignation. We call it "being realistic" or "mature" or "responsible." We give people participation trophies for staying in situations that are slowly killing them.

"At least you have a job." "At least you're not divorced." "At least you're not dead."

See what I mean? We're so addicted to the "At Least" reflex that we've convinced ourselves that not being miserable is the same as being happy.

It's not.

Path Three: Reframing

This is the path almost nobody takes because it requires actual work.

Reframing means you look at the same shitty situation everyone else is looking at, but you ask a different question.

Not "Why is this happening to me?" (that's Reaction)

Not "I guess this is just how life is" (that's Resignation)

But "What can I learn from this that will make me stronger?"

I know. That sounds like something you'd read on a motivational poster next to a picture of a bald eagle. But stay with me.

When my wife had her first seizure, my immediate reaction was terror. Then came weeks of resignation—"I guess we're just medical crisis people now."

But eventually, I reframed. This wasn't happening to me; it was happening for me. It was showing me what actually matters. It was teaching me how to be present. It was forcing me to stop taking her for granted.

Did that make the seizures fun? Hell no. But it made them bearable. And more than that, it made them meaningful.

* * *

How to Actually Break the Pattern (Not Just Think About It)

Okay, so you've identified your pattern. You know you keep dating emotionally unavailable people, or sabotaging yourself at work, or spending money you don't have, or whatever your particular flavor of self-destruction looks like.

Now what?

Here's the uncomfortable truth: knowing about the pattern doesn't break it. You can be fully aware that you're doing the same stupid thing you've done a hundred times before, and you'll still do it again.

That's because patterns live in your nervous system, not your brain. They're habits, and habits don't care about your insights or intentions. They only respond to new behavior, repeated consistently, over time.

So if you want to break a pattern, you need to do three things:

First: Catch yourself in the act.

This is harder than it sounds. Patterns are automatic, which means you're usually halfway through the old behavior before you even realize you're doing it.

The trick is to identify the trigger—the specific situation, emotion, or thought that kicks off the pattern. For my friend with the three divorces, his trigger was feeling criticized. Any time his partner said something that felt even remotely like criticism, he'd shut down emotionally and stop communicating. Which, of course, made his partner feel unheard, which led to more criticism, which made him shut down harder. Rinse, repeat, divorce.

Once you know your trigger, you can start catching yourself before you go all the way down the pattern rabbit hole.

Second: Pause before you proceed.

This is where most people fail. They catch themselves starting the pattern, but then they do it anyway because it feels too uncomfortable to stop.

You need to build in a pause—a literal moment where you stop and ask yourself, "Do I want to keep doing this, or do I want to try something different?"

The pause doesn't have to be long. Five seconds. Ten seconds. Just long enough to break the automaticity.

Deep breath. Count to three. Ask the question. Then choose.

Third: Pick a different path—just this once.

Don't try to fix everything at once. Don't commit to never doing the pattern again. That's too big, and your brain will sabotage you.

Instead, just commit to doing something different this one time.

Your partner says something that feels critical? Instead of shutting down, try saying, "That hurt my feelings. Can we talk about it?"

You're about to stress-eat a whole pizza? Instead, go for a walk first. If you still want the pizza after the walk, fine. But try the walk first.

You're about to say yes to something you don't want to do? Try saying, "Let me think about it and get back to you." Just this once.

That's it. Catch, pause, choose differently. One time.

Then do it again tomorrow. And the day after that. And eventually—not immediately, not magically, but eventually—the new behavior becomes the new pattern.

* * *

The Hard Part (Because There's Always a Hard Part)

Here's what nobody tells you about breaking patterns: it will feel wrong at first.

Not hard. Not difficult. Wrong.

Because remember, your brain equates "familiar" with "safe." So when you do something unfamiliar—even if it's objectively better for you—your brain freaks out.

Setting boundaries with your toxic family member will feel mean, even though it's not.

Saving money instead of spending it will feel boring, even though it's responsible.

Choosing to work out instead of scrolling through social media will feel like you're missing out, even though you're not.

That discomfort is not a sign that you're doing it wrong. It's a sign that you're doing it right.

Your job is to sit with that discomfort and keep going anyway.

Not because it's easy—it won't be—but because every time you choose Path Three, you're building the muscle that will eventually make happiness your default instead of your exception.

And that, my friend, is how you stop being a victim of life and start being someone who actually controls it.

Now go practice.

# Chapter 4 When Life Falls Apart: The Asset Audit

September 2017. Hurricane Irma.

Not the actual storm—that part was almost manageable. We evacuated, stayed with family, rode it out like everyone else in Florida. Scary but survivable.

The real disaster came three weeks later when Izzy had her first grand mal seizure on our living room floor.

She was fine one second—laughing at something on her phone—and the next second she was on the ground, convulsing, eyes rolled back, making sounds I'd never heard a human make. I thought she was dying. I was sure she was dying.

She wasn't. But our life as we knew it? That died.

No more driving for her. No more independence. No more assuming she'd be safe if I left the room for five minutes. Every plan we'd made—vacation we'd booked, jobs she'd applied for, the casual assumption that tomorrow would look basically like today—all of it instantly obsolete.

And here's what nobody tells you about catastrophic life changes: they don't come with instructions.

There's no manual titled "What to Do When Your World Explodes." There's just you, standing in the wreckage, trying to figure out if you're supposed to cry or clean up or both.

I chose both. And then I chose something else.

* * *

The Loss List (Or: Everything That Just Died)

In the weeks after Izzy's diagnosis, I made a list. Not because I'm some kind of masochist, but because I needed to understand the full scope of what we'd lost. You can't grieve something properly if you're pretending it didn't matter.

Here's what we lost:

Independence. Izzy couldn't drive anymore. Couldn't be alone. Couldn't do the thousand small things that make you feel like an adult instead of a patient.

Spontaneity. Every activity now required planning, risk assessment, backup plans. "Let's go to the beach" became "Let's research which beaches have EMS response times under 10 minutes."

Career trajectory. The jobs Izzy had been applying for? All required driving. All required being alone sometimes. All suddenly impossible.

Sleep. I developed this lovely habit of waking up every two hours to make sure she was still breathing. Seizures can happen in your sleep. Did you know that? I do now.

Certainty. We'd always operated on the assumption that we were basically healthy people. That assumption died on our living room floor along with a bunch of others.

The future we'd planned. Not just the vacation we'd booked or the weekend trips we'd talked about. The whole blueprint. "Someday we'll do this" became "maybe never."

That's a pretty brutal list. And if I'd stopped there—if I'd just catalogued the losses and called it a day—I would have drowned in it.

But I didn't stop there.

* * *

The Asset Audit (Or: What You Gain When Everything Falls Apart)

About a month after the seizure—after the initial panic subsided, after we'd found neurologists and medications and established new routines—I started a second list.

This one was harder to write because it required me to acknowledge something uncomfortable: catastrophe had given me things.

Not that I was grateful for the seizure—fuck that toxic positivity nonsense. I'd gladly give back every "gift" if it meant Izzy could drive again. But the gifts existed whether I wanted them or not, and pretending they didn't exist felt like wasting them.

So I called it an Asset Audit. Like a financial audit, but for your life after disaster. What assets do you now possess that you didn't have before?

Here's what I found:

Asset #1: Clarity

Nothing clarifies your priorities like watching your wife seize. All the petty workplace drama, the manufactured urgency, the things I'd been stressed about the day before—they evaporated instantly. I now knew exactly what mattered and what didn't. That's not a small thing.

Asset #2: Presence

Before the seizure, I was one of those people who's physically present but mentally somewhere else. Always planning the next thing, replaying the last thing, never fully here. After? I couldn't afford that luxury anymore. When you don't know if your wife is going to have another seizure, you pay attention. You're present. You notice.

Turns out, presence is an actual skill you can develop, and crisis is an excellent teacher.

Asset #3: Resilience (The Real Kind)

I used to think resilience meant "bouncing back." Like a rubber band that returns to its original shape after being stretched. But that's not how it works with real catastrophe. You don't bounce back. You break, and then you rebuild yourself into something different.

The me that existed before September 2017 couldn't have handled what came after. But I became someone who could. That's not bouncing back. That's evolution.

Asset #4: Empathy at Scale

Before Izzy's diagnosis, I thought I was empathetic. I wasn't. I was sympathetic, which is different. Sympathy is "I'm sorry that happened to you." Empathy is "I know what that feels like because I've been there too."

Now when someone tells me their life fell apart, I don't just feel bad for them. I know. I know the specific terror of watching your future disappear. I know the exhaustion of rebuilding from nothing. I know the weird guilt of finding gifts in the wreckage.

That's an asset. A painful one, but an asset nonetheless.

Asset #5: A Better Marriage

This one's going to sound insane, but it's true: Izzy's seizures made our marriage better.

Not because trauma is romantic (it's not) or because suffering brings people together (it usually doesn't). But because crisis burns away all the bullshit. We couldn't afford to be petty anymore. Couldn't afford to hold grudges or play games or communicate passive-aggressively.

We had to be honest, direct, and present with each other. All the time. Or the relationship wouldn't survive.

So we became honest, direct, and present. And our marriage got better.

Again—would I trade that for her being healthy? Absolutely. But I'm not allowed to make that trade, so I might as well acknowledge what we gained.

* * *

How to Do Your Own Asset Audit (Without Lying to Yourself)

Okay, so you've had something terrible happen. Maybe it's medical like mine, maybe it's financial, maybe it's relational. Maybe your world just exploded and you're standing in the rubble trying to figure out what the hell comes next.

Here's what you do:

Step One: Make the Loss List

Do not skip this step. I'm serious.

You cannot do an honest Asset Audit if you haven't first acknowledged what you lost. If you try to jump straight to "what did I gain," you're just doing toxic positivity in disguise. You're telling yourself to "look on the bright side" when what you actually need to do is grieve.

So make the list. Everything that died when your life fell apart. Be specific. Be honest. Be as brutal as you need to be.

Don't worry about being grateful yet. Don't worry about finding the silver lining. Just inventory the damage.

Step Two: Give Yourself Permission to Grieve

Once you've made the Loss List, actually feel the losses. Cry about them if you need to. Get angry. Punch a pillow. Scream in your car. Whatever works.

This isn't wallowing. This is processing. There's a difference.

Wallowing is when you revisit the same painful thoughts over and over without moving through them. Processing is when you let yourself feel the full weight of what you lost, acknowledge that it hurts, and then—eventually—start looking for what comes next.

How long does this take? However long it takes. Could be days, could be months. There's no timeline.

Step Three: Start the Asset Audit

Only after you've grieved—not before, not instead of—can you start looking for assets.

And here's the key: you're not looking for things to be grateful for. You're looking for things you now possess that you didn't have before.

Assets. Resources. Capabilities. Skills. Perspectives.

Some will be obvious. "I now possess the ability to set boundaries because I learned the hard way what happens when I don't." "I now possess clarity about my priorities because crisis burned away everything that didn't matter."

Some will be uncomfortable. "I now possess knowledge of my own capacity for survival." "I now possess firsthand understanding of what it's like to rebuild from nothing."

Write them all down. The comfortable ones and the uncomfortable ones.

Step Four: Use the Assets

This is where most people fuck it up.

They make the list, acknowledge the assets, feel briefly better... and then do nothing with them. They treat the Asset Audit like a mental exercise instead of a blueprint for reconstruction.

Don't do that.

If you've gained clarity about your priorities, restructure your life around those priorities.

If you've gained the ability to be present, practice that presence daily.

If you've gained empathy, use it to help others who are going through what you went through.

The assets are only valuable if you deploy them.

* * *

The Part Nobody Wants to Hear (But I'm Going to Say It Anyway)

Here's the uncomfortable truth about catastrophe:

You don't get to choose whether it happens.

You only get to choose what you do with it.

I didn't choose for Izzy to have seizures. She didn't choose it. It just happened, like hurricanes happen, like accidents happen, like every terrible thing that's ever happened to anyone.

But I did choose how to respond.

I could have chosen Reaction—panic, blame, resentment, rage. God knows I felt all of those things. I could have stayed there.

I could have chosen Resignation—"I guess we're just medical crisis people now." I could have let it define us, limit us, become the only story we ever told about ourselves.

Instead, I chose Reframing. Which meant I had to look at the same shitty situation everyone else was looking at and ask a different question.

Not "Why did this happen to us?" (unanswerable, useless)

Not "How do we get back to normal?" (impossible, pointless)

But "What can we build with what we have left?"

That's the Asset Audit question. That's the only question that matters after disaster.

Because you can't un-break what's broken. You can't go back to who you were before. That person doesn't exist anymore.

But you can inventory what you have left—including the things you gained in the breaking—and start building something new.

It won't be the life you planned. It might not even be the life you wanted.

But it will be yours. And it will be real. And that's enough to start with.

So do the audit. Grieve what's gone. Acknowledge what you gained. And then get to work building whatever comes next.

Because you're not a victim of your circumstances.

You're an architect with new materials.

Now build something.

# Chapter 5 Turning Loss into Legacy: When Death Takes Someone You Need

My mom had a stroke on a Tuesday.

I remember that because I'd just finished teaching a corporate training on resilience. Literally walked off stage from telling a room full of executives how to bounce back from adversity, checked my phone, and saw seventeen missed calls from my brother.

The universe has a dark sense of humor.

She survived the stroke, which sounds like good news until you understand that "survived" doesn't mean "recovered." The woman who came home from the hospital wasn't the woman who'd raised me. That woman was gone. In her place was someone who looked like my mom but couldn't remember my name half the time.

She lived another eight months. Eight months of watching her fade a little more each day. Eight months of having the same conversation three times in an hour because her short-term memory was Swiss cheese. Eight months of seeing the recognition in her eyes dim until one day it just... stopped.

And then she died.

Not dramatically. Not peacefully-in-her-sleep like they show in movies. She just stopped breathing on a random Thursday while my brother was in the room. Her body gave up, and that was it.

No last words. No final moment of clarity. No Hollywood ending.

Just gone.

* * *

What Nobody Tells You About Grief

Here's what they don't put in the sympathy cards:

Grief isn't sad. It's empty.

Sadness has texture, has depth, has something to hold onto. Grief is the absence of all that. It's walking around with a hole in your chest where a person used to be, and everyone expects you to just... function normally?

After my mom died, people kept telling me, "She's in a better place." Like that was supposed to help. Like knowing she wasn't suffering anymore would fill the hole.

It didn't.

They told me, "Time heals all wounds." Which is bullshit. Time doesn't heal anything—it just changes your relationship with the wound. You learn to carry it. Some days it's a dull ache. Some days it's a knife in the ribs for no reason.

They told me, "She'd want you to be happy." Maybe. Probably. But she's dead, so what she wants is kind of irrelevant now, isn't it?

The worst part? The absolute worst part?

Life keeps going.

Bills still need to be paid. Work still needs to be done. Your wife still needs you to remember to take out the trash. The world doesn't stop spinning just because someone fell off.

And you're supposed to just... adapt. Move on. Get over it.

Except you don't get over it. You don't move on.

You just get different.

* * *

The Thing Grief Steals That Nobody Talks About

About three months after my mom died, I had this realization that gutted me all over again:

I couldn't call her anymore.

I know. Obvious, right? She's dead, of course you can't call her. But it's not just about the phone calls.

It's about the fact that I'd never get to tell her about anything ever again. Never share a funny story. Never ask for advice. Never hear her laugh at one of my stupid jokes.

All the future moments we'd never have—those died too.

She'd never meet any grandchildren I might have. Never see me accomplish anything else. Never know how the story ends.

And that's the thing grief steals that nobody prepares you for: it takes the future, not just the past.

You lose the person, yes. But you also lose every version of tomorrow that included them. Every holiday. Every milestone. Every random Tuesday when you would have just... talked.

That's the second death. The one that happens slowly, over years, as you accumulate moments they should have been in but weren't.

* * *

The Question Nobody Wants to Ask (But I'm Going to Ask It Anyway)

About six months after my mom died, I was sitting in my car in a parking lot—don't remember why, doesn't matter—and I asked myself the question everyone thinks but nobody says out loud:

What's the point of loving people if they're just going to die?

I'm serious. If you know—know—that everyone you love is going to die eventually, why bother? Why set yourself up for that kind of pain?

Why build a life with someone knowing you'll either lose them or they'll lose you?

Why have kids knowing you'll watch them suffer and struggle and eventually die too?

Why make friends, invest in relationships, care about anything or anyone when the ending is always the same?

I sat in that parking lot for twenty minutes wrestling with that question. And then I had a second realization, which was even worse:

The alternative is worse.

Because the alternative to loving people who die is... what? Not loving anyone? Going through life emotionally disconnected so you never have to grieve?

That's not safety. That's death by another name.

So here's the uncomfortable truth I landed on: the pain of loss is the price of admission for having loved someone. You don't get one without the other.

Which means the question isn't "How do I avoid grief?"

It's "What do I do with it?"

* * *

Turning Loss Into Legacy (The Only Thing That Actually Helps)

About a year after my mom died, I was cleaning out her house—the final purge, getting it ready to sell—and I found a box of letters she'd saved.

Letters from me, from when I was a kid at summer camp. Stupid stuff. "Dear Mom, today we went canoeing and I fell in the lake. The food here sucks. Love, Ken."

She'd kept every single one. Twenty-plus years of dumb letters from a kid who took her for granted.

And I realized: this is what she left behind. Not just memories in my head, but evidence of her love. Tangible proof that she cared enough to save stupid letters that meant nothing to anyone but her.

That's a legacy.

Not some grand gesture or world-changing achievement. Just a box of letters that proved someone loved me.

And that's when I understood what turning loss into legacy actually means. It's not about erasing the grief or "honoring their memory" with some performative bullshit. It's about finding the thing they gave you—the lesson, the trait, the value, the habit—and carrying it forward.

Here's what my mom gave me:

Persistence. My mom was a fighter. Not in the aggressive sense, but in the "I'm not giving up even when everything sucks" sense. Watching her recover from that stroke—knowing she'd never fully recover but still showing up to physical therapy every damn day—that taught me what real resilience looks like.

Now when I want to quit something because it's hard, I think about her dragging herself to therapy when she could barely walk. And I keep going.

Presence. Even after the stroke, even when she couldn't remember my name, she was still there when I visited. She'd light up—not because she knew who I was, but because someone was paying attention to her. That taught me something about showing up that I didn't understand before.

Now I make it a point to actually be present when I'm with people. Not scrolling my phone. Not half-listening. There. Because that's what she gave me, even at the end.

The ability to hold pain without being destroyed by it. This one took me a long time to understand. My mom had a hard life. Multiple divorces. Financial struggles. Health problems. But she didn't let those things make her bitter or cynical or mean.

She carried her pain without becoming it. And that's a skill I'm still learning, but I'm learning it because she showed me it's possible.

Those are my inheritances. Not money or property—she didn't have much of that. But persistence, presence, and the capacity to endure without breaking.

That's her legacy. And every time I use one of those traits, she's alive again for a moment.

* * *

How to Build a Legacy From Loss (A Framework, Not a Formula)

Okay, so someone you love died. Maybe it was sudden. Maybe it was slow. Maybe you had time to say goodbye, maybe you didn't. Doesn't matter—they're gone either way.

And now you're standing in the wreckage trying to figure out what comes next.

Here's what doesn't help: platitudes. "Everything happens for a reason." "They're in a better place." "God needed another angel."

Fuck that noise.

Here's what does help: finding the thing they gave you and choosing to keep it alive.

Not as a memorial. Not as obligation. But as inheritance.

Here's how:

Step One: Grieve first. Legacy later.

Do not—I repeat, do not—try to turn grief into something meaningful while you're still in the thick of it. That's not processing; that's avoiding.

You need to sit with the emptiness first. Feel the full weight of the loss. Cry. Rage. Break things if you need to (within reason—don't get arrested).

The legacy work comes later, after you've acknowledged that this person is actually, permanently gone.

Step Two: Identify what they gave you.

Not what they did for you. Not what they bought you or how they supported you logistically.

What they gave you. What part of who you are came from them?

Maybe it's a sense of humor. Maybe it's work ethic. Maybe it's the ability to cook a specific dish or fix a specific problem. Maybe it's just the way they taught you to treat people.

Find that thing. Name it. Own it.

Step Three: Deploy it deliberately.

Once you've identified what they gave you, the work is to use it. Consciously. Repeatedly.

Not because you owe them. Not because you're trying to keep their memory alive. But because it's yours now, and it would be a waste not to use it.

My mom taught me persistence? I'm going to be persistent. Not for her. For me. Because that's what I inherited, and inheritances are meant to be spent.

Step Four: Pass it on.

This is the part that turns inheritance into legacy.

Whatever they gave you, give it to someone else. Teach it. Model it. Share it. Don't let it die with you.

That's how people become immortal. Not through statues or monuments, but through the ripples they create in other people's lives.

My mom's persistence lives in me. And when I teach my nephew to keep going when things are hard, it lives in him too. And when he teaches his kids someday, it'll live in them. Even on her deathbed, her last couple of months on this earth I met with her daily to help her finish the last couple of books she wanted done so I could publish them for her. You'll learn about those projects and her determination to finish them. She even had me writing for her on her last day alive.

She's been dead for years, since 2018, but her legacy is still expanding.

That's the only thing that makes death even slightly bearable.

* * *

The Uncomfortable Truth About Death (That Makes Life Worth Living)

Here's the thing nobody wants to acknowledge:

Death is what makes life matter.

If we lived forever, nothing would be urgent. Nothing would be precious. You could always do it tomorrow, see them next year, say the thing eventually.

But we don't live forever. We get a limited number of days, and we don't know how many, and that scarcity is what gives life its weight.

Every conversation with someone you love could be the last one. Every meal. Every laugh. Every mundane Tuesday.

That's not depressing. That's clarifying.

Because if you really internalize that—if you really let yourself feel the finite nature of everything—you stop wasting time on bullshit.

You stop holding grudges over petty things. You stop delaying the important conversations. You stop taking people for granted.

Not because you're morbid or obsessed with death, but because you understand the math: you have limited time with everyone you love, and you don't get to know the expiration date in advance.

So, you show up. You pay attention. You say the things that need to be said. You love people while you can.

And when they die—because they will, eventually—you'll still grieve. You'll still have the hole in your chest. You'll still wish you had more time.

But you won't have regrets about the time you did have.

And that's the best anyone can hope for.

So grieve when you need to grieve. Feel the emptiness. Acknowledge the loss.

And then—when you're ready, not before—find what they gave you and carry it forward.

Because that's what turns loss into legacy.

That's what makes death bearable.

And that's what makes the limited time we have with people worth the inevitable pain of losing them.

Love anyway. Grieve when you must. Carry them forward.

# Chapter 6 The Personal Relationship Reframe: When the People Who Should Love You Are the Ones Destroying You

Before We Talk About Toxic People: What If YOU'RE the Problem?

Let's start with the most uncomfortable question first, because if I don't, you'll spend this entire chapter nodding along thinking, "Yes! Everyone else in my life is the problem!"

And maybe they are. Maybe you're surrounded by genuinely awful people who drain your energy and treat you like garbage.

Or maybe—just maybe—you're the common denominator.

Here's how to tell the difference:

If ONE person in your life treats you badly, that's their problem. If EVERYONE in your life treats you badly, that's your problem. Because either you're choosing terrible people, or you're training people to treat you terribly, or both.

So before we go any further, do a quick gut check:

Do you set boundaries, or do you just resent people for crossing boundaries you never actually stated?

Do you communicate your needs clearly, or do you expect people to read your mind and then get mad when they can't?

Do you take responsibility for your part in conflicts, or is it always someone else's fault?

Do you choose people who are actually capable of healthy relationships, or do you keep going for the same broken type hoping this time will be different?

If you're honest with yourself and the answer to most of those questions is "Oh shit, I might be the problem," then good. That's actually great news. Because you can fix you. You can't fix other people.

But if you're honest with yourself and the answer is "No, I do all those things and people still treat me like garbage," then keep reading. This chapter is for you.

* * *

Story One: The Thanksgiving Massacre (Or: When Family Is the Toxin)

Thanksgiving, 2014. My first holiday with Izzy's extended family.

Izzy has this aunt—let's call her Karen because that's what she is—who's one of those people who thinks "brutal honesty" is a personality trait instead of just being cruel with plausible deniability.

We're sitting at dinner. Everything's fine. And then Karen looks at Izzy and says, loud enough for the whole table to hear: "You know, you'd be so pretty if you just lost about fifteen pounds."

The table goes silent.

Izzy's face does that thing where she's trying not to cry but her eyes are already wet. And what do I do? What does her brave, protective husband do in this moment?

Nothing.

I sit there like a coward and stuff mashed potatoes in my face because confrontation is uncomfortable and it's a family dinner and I don't want to make things weird.

Izzy excuses herself to the bathroom. Karen keeps eating like she didn't just publicly humiliate someone. Everyone else pretends it didn't happen.

And that's how the rest of dinner goes. Izzy barely talks. I feel like garbage. Karen seems pleased with herself.

Later, in the car, Izzy is silent. Not crying anymore—past that. Just... empty.

Finally she says, "You didn't say anything."

And I know exactly what she means, but I play dumb anyway. "About what?"

"About Karen. She humiliated me in front of everyone, and you just sat there."

I start making excuses. "I didn't want to make a scene." "It's family, you know how she is." "She didn't mean it that way."

And Izzy looks at me—really looks at me—and says something I'll never forget:

"You weren't even in the stadium."

I don't understand at first, so she explains: "When someone attacks me, I need you in the stadium. I don't even need you to fight for me—just be there. Show up. Let me know I'm not alone. But you weren't even in the stadium. You were outside in the parking lot pretending nothing was happening."

And she was right.

That night, I realized something: toxic people don't just hurt the people they target. They hurt everyone who enables them by staying silent.

And I'd been an enabler.

The Asset Audit From That Night:

After that disaster, I gained something I didn't have before: clarity about what "being in the stadium" actually means. It's not about being aggressive or starting fights. It's about showing up for the people you love when someone hurts them. Even if it's uncomfortable. Especially if it's uncomfortable.

The next family gathering, Karen made another comment. This time, I was in the stadium. I said, calmly but clearly, "That's not okay. Don't talk to my wife that way."

Did it make things awkward? Absolutely. Did Karen pitch a fit about "not being able to joke anymore"? You bet. Did she ever make another comment like that? Nope.

Because toxic people rely on your silence. Once you break it, they lose their power.

* * *

Story Two: The Critical Father (Or: When "Helping" Is Actually Sabotage)

I have a friend—we'll call him Dave—whose father has perfected the art of the undermining compliment.

Dave gets a promotion at work. His dad's response? "That's great! Now you just need to work on your presentation skills so they don't regret promoting you."

Dave buys a house. His dad's response? "Nice place. Shame about the neighborhood. Property values probably won't appreciate much here."

Dave gets engaged. His dad's response? "She seems lovely. Are you sure you're ready for marriage though? You've always had trouble with commitment."

Every single achievement, every milestone, every moment of pride—his father found a way to inject criticism disguised as concern.

And here's the insidious part: Dave's dad genuinely thought he was helping. In his mind, he was "keeping Dave humble" and "preparing him for reality" and "making sure he didn't get complacent."

What he was actually doing was teaching Dave that nothing he ever did would be good enough.

Dave spent decades trying to earn his father's unqualified approval. New job, bigger house, better car, more impressive accomplishments. Didn't matter. His dad always found the flaw.

Then one day, at 34 years old, Dave had a breakthrough. He'd just closed the biggest deal of his career—something that would legitimately change his company's trajectory. He called his dad to share the news.

His dad's response? "That's impressive. Just remember, the bigger the success, the harder the fall. Don't get overconfident."

And Dave, for the first time in his life, said: "You know what, Dad? I'm not doing this anymore."

"Doing what?"

"Waiting for you to be happy for me. I just accomplished something huge, and instead of celebrating with me, you're already preparing me for failure. I'm done chasing your approval. You can offer it or not—that's your choice. But I'm done letting your inability to celebrate determine my self-worth."

And then he hung up.

His dad called back two hours later, offended, demanding to know why Dave was "being so sensitive."

Dave didn't answer. He was busy celebrating with people who could actually be happy for him.

The Asset Audit From Dave's Breakthrough:

What Dave gained that day: permission to stop performing for an audience that would never applaud. He realized that some people are constitutionally incapable of celebrating you, and continuing to seek their validation is like trying to get blood from a stone—you'll just hurt yourself trying.

His relationship with his father didn't improve. But Dave's relationship with himself did. He stopped measuring his worth by his dad's impossible standards and started measuring it by his own values.

That's the reframe: you can't change critical people, but you can change whose opinion you let matter.

* * *

Story Three: Sarah (Or: When Love Becomes Surveillance)

Before Izzy, I dated someone we'll call Sarah. Three-year relationship. Started great, ended in a dumpster fire that I should have seen coming from miles away.

Year one was amazing. Sarah was attentive, thoughtful, always wanted to spend time together. I thought I'd hit the relationship jackpot.

Year two, things shifted. "Attentive" became "intrusive." "Thoughtful" became "controlling." "Always wanting to spend time together" became "not letting me spend time with anyone else."

She wanted to know where I was at all times. Not in a cute "I miss you" way—in a "if you don't text me back within 10 minutes I'm calling your friends to find you" way.

She wanted passwords to my email and social media "because couples who trust each other don't hide anything."

She got upset if I made plans without checking with her first. Even if it was just grabbing lunch with a coworker.

And here's the really messed up part: she framed all of this as love. "I just care about you so much." "I just want to be close to you." "I just want to make sure you're safe."

But it wasn't love. It was ownership disguised as affection.

Year three was when it got really bad. She started threatening self-harm whenever I tried to set boundaries. "If you go out with your friends tonight, I don't know what I'll do." Translation: I'm holding myself hostage to control your behavior.

She created fake social media accounts to check if I was flirting with anyone online. (I wasn't. But that didn't stop her from accusing me based on her spy work.)

She showed up unannounced at my apartment, my job, my gym—"just wanted to surprise you!"—but really just wanted to make sure I was where I said I'd be.

I knew it was bad. I knew I needed to leave. But I was trapped in that classic abusive relationship logic: "If I just love her better, she'll stop being like this." "If I just reassure her enough, she'll feel secure." "If I just prove I'm loyal, she'll learn to trust me."

Spoiler alert: none of that worked. Because the problem wasn't my behavior—it was hers. And you can't fix someone else's dysfunction with your compliance.

The relationship ended when I finally grew a spine and broke up with her. She sent me 47 texts in one hour. Called from different numbers when I blocked her. Showed up at my apartment and had to be escorted away by building security.

Not a fun breakup.

The Asset Audit From That Nightmare:

What I gained from three years with Sarah: a finely tuned radar for controlling behavior. I can spot the red flags now from a mile away. Someone who needs constant reassurance? Flag. Someone who gets upset about you having friends? Flag. Someone who monitors your phone? Massive flag.

I also learned that "I love you" doesn't excuse bad behavior. Love that requires you to shrink yourself, isolate yourself, or constantly prove yourself isn't love. It's control with better marketing.

And most importantly: I learned that you can't fix broken people by staying with them. They have to want to fix themselves. Your job is to protect yourself, not rehabilitate them.

* * *

How to Actually Set Boundaries (With Specific Scripts You Can Use)

Okay, so you've identified the toxic people in your life. You've done the uncomfortable self-audit and determined you're not the problem (or you've fixed your part of the problem). Now what?

Now you set boundaries. But not vague, wishy-washy boundaries that leave room for interpretation. Clear, specific boundaries with consequences.

Here's the formula:

"When you [specific behavior], I feel [specific emotion]. Going forward, I need [specific change]. If that doesn't happen, I will [specific consequence]."

Let's apply this to our three stories:

For Karen (The Toxic Family Member):

"Karen, when you make comments about Izzy's weight or appearance, it hurts her and makes family gatherings uncomfortable. Going forward, I need you to keep those thoughts to yourself. If you make another comment like that, we'll leave, and we won't be attending future family events where you're present."

Notice what this does: names the behavior, states the impact, requires a change, specifies the consequence. No wiggle room.

For Dave's Dad (The Critical Parent):

"Dad, when you respond to my successes with criticism, it makes me not want to share things with you. Going forward, I need you to celebrate with me or stay silent. If you can't do that, I'll stop telling you about my life, and our relationship will be limited to surface-level conversations."

Again: behavior, impact, requirement, consequence.

For Sarah (The Controlling Partner):

"Sarah, when you demand my passwords and track my location, it makes me feel like I'm being surveilled instead of loved. Going forward, I need you to respect my privacy and trust me without constant verification. If that's not possible, this relationship can't continue."

Same structure. Crystal clear.

Here's What Will Happen When You Set Boundaries:

The toxic person will push back. They'll tell you you're overreacting, being too sensitive, taking things too seriously. They'll accuse you of not caring about them, of being selfish, of changing for the worse.

This is normal. This is their last attempt to maintain control. Don't cave.

Repeat your boundary. Enforce your consequence. And then watch what happens.

One of two things will occur:

Option One: They'll adjust their behavior because they value the relationship more than they value being toxic. (This is rare but does happen.)

Option Two: They'll double down on their toxicity, violate the boundary again, and force you to enforce the consequence. Which means they've chosen to lose access to you.

Either way, you win. Because you're no longer tolerating behavior that damages you.

Setting boundaries with people you love—family, partners, lifelong friends—is one of the hardest things you'll ever do. It feels mean. It feels selfish. It feels like you're destroying the relationship.

But here's the truth: if a boundary destroys the relationship, the relationship was already broken.

You're just making the brokenness visible.

And that's painful. But it's also necessary.

Because the alternative is spending your life accommodating people who hurt you, shrinking yourself to make them comfortable, and pretending that's love.

It's not love. It's surrender.

Set the boundaries. Enforce the consequences. Protect yourself.

The people who love you will adjust. The people who don't will leave.

Let them.

# Chapter 7 The Social Battlefield: How to Survive Friendships That Drain You and Workplaces That Want Your Soul

Here's the difference between Chapter 6 and Chapter 7:

Chapter 6 was about the people you're supposed to love—family, romantic partners, the relationships that come with the weight of obligation and history.

Chapter 7 is about everyone else. The friends you chose (or thought you chose). The coworkers you're stuck with eight hours a day. The professional relationships that determine whether you get promoted or plateaued.

These relationships are messier because the rules are less clear. Family toxicity is obvious—you can point to it and say "that's my abusive father" and people nod sympathetically. Workplace toxicity is subtle. Friendship toxicity is invisible.

Until it destroys you.

* * *

Story One: Marcus (Or: The 15-Year Friendship That Was Actually Slow-Motion Sabotage)

I had a best friend for fifteen years. We'll call him Marcus.

Met him in college. Stayed close through our twenties and thirties. Did all the friendship things—fantasy football leagues, bachelor party planning, being each other's emergency contacts. I would have told you, confidently, that Marcus was one of the most important people in my life.

And then, when I was 35, my wife threw me a surprise birthday party.

Marcus showed up late—not unusual for him. What was unusual was what he said when he arrived.

I'm talking to a group of friends, telling some dumb story about work, and Marcus walks up mid-story. Doesn't wait for me to finish. Just interrupts with:

"Oh, is this the story where Ken pretends he saved the project when really it was the whole team? Because I've heard this one before."

The group laughs—awkwardly, because nobody's sure if he's joking or being a dick. I laugh too, because what else do you do?

But it keeps happening all night.

Someone asks about my new promotion. Marcus: "Yeah, must be nice having connections. Rest of us actually have to earn it."

Someone compliments the party Izzy threw. Marcus: "She's good at this stuff. Ken would have just ordered pizza and called it a day."

Every single thing—every conversation, every achievement, every moment—he found a way to diminish it.

And here's the insidious part: he did it with a smile. Always joking. Always "just messing with you, man." Always plausible deniability if anyone called him out.

After the party, Izzy said something that broke me:

"I don't think Marcus likes you very much."

I defended him immediately. "He's just like that. It's his sense of humor. We've been friends for fifteen years—of course he likes me."

She looked at me with that expression wives get when they know something you don't want to admit. "Okay. When's the last time he celebrated something good that happened to you?"

I started to answer and... couldn't.

"When's the last time he asked about your life without making it about himself?"

Couldn't answer that either.

"When's the last time you hung out and felt better afterward instead of worse?"

Silence.

And then she asked the question that destroyed fifteen years of friendship:

"If you stopped initiating contact, how long do you think it would take before he reached out to you?"

I was sure she was wrong. Marcus was my best friend. Of course he'd reach out.

So I tested it.

Stopped texting first. Stopped calling. Stopped making plans.

And I waited.

Three months went by. Not a single text. Not a call. Not even a "hey man, you alive?"

Fifteen years of friendship, and it took three months of silence for me to realize: I wasn't his friend. I was his audience.

Someone to listen to his problems. Someone to make him feel better about himself by comparison. Someone to diminish so he could feel bigger.

That's not friendship. That's parasitism with nostalgia.

The Asset Audit From Losing Marcus:

What I gained from that loss: clarity about what actual friendship looks like. Real friends celebrate your wins. Real friends ask about your life without making it about themselves. Real friends reach out, not just respond.

I also learned that longevity doesn't equal quality. Fifteen years sounds impressive, but fifteen years of being someone's emotional punching bag is nothing to be proud of.

And most importantly: I learned that you're allowed to end friendships that don't serve you. There's no friendship police that's going to arrest you for stopping contact with someone who makes you feel like shit.

I didn't send Marcus a breakup text. Didn't have a dramatic confrontation. Just... stopped performing the friendship. And he never noticed.

That told me everything I needed to know.

* * *

Story Two: Diane (Or: The Boss Who Assassinated You With Compliments)

My second corporate job out of grad school, I worked for a woman named Diane. She was smart, articulate, well-connected. Everyone loved her.

And for the first six months, I thought she was great.

She'd praise me in meetings. Tell other departments how lucky she was to have me on her team. Write glowing performance reviews. From the outside, it looked like I was crushing it.

But behind closed doors, she was systematically destroying my career.

Here's how it worked:

I'd pitch an idea in our one-on-one meetings. She'd say it was brilliant, tell me to develop it, even assign resources to help. Then, in the next leadership meeting, she'd present my idea as hers. I'd find out later from colleagues—"Hey, great idea you had about the client retention strategy!" Except I never presented it. She did.

When I brought it up with her, she'd act confused. "Oh, I thought we developed that together? I must have misremembered. You know how collaborative our team is!"

Or she'd assign me high-visibility projects, let me do all the work, and then "collaborate" at the last minute—which meant she'd swoop in, make minor changes, and take credit during the presentation to executives.

Or—and this was her specialty—she'd praise me publicly while quietly blocking my advancement opportunities. I'd apply for promotions or lateral moves, thinking she'd support me given all the positive feedback. But then I'd hear through the grapevine that she'd told the hiring managers I "wasn't ready yet" or "still had areas to develop" or "might not be the right culture fit."

All while telling me to my face that I was doing amazing work.

I spent fifteen months in this gaslighting nightmare. Fifteen months thinking I was losing my mind. Because how could someone who praised me so publicly be sabotaging me so privately?

The truth came out at a company happy hour.

One of the VPs—a guy named Tom who'd had too many drinks—pulled me aside and said, "You know

Diane's blocking your transfer to the innovation team, right?"

I didn't know. I'd applied for that position three months earlier. Diane told me I was a finalist but ultimately they "went in a different direction."

Tom kept talking, drunk and honest: "Yeah, she told the hiring manager you were too green. Said she was worried you'd fail and it would reflect poorly on her team. But man, I've seen your work—you're better than half the people in that department. She's just scared you'll outshine her."

And there it was. The truth I'd been too naive to see:

Diane didn't want me to succeed. She wanted me to stay just successful enough to make her look good, but never successful enough to threaten her position.

I quit two weeks later. No dramatic exit. No confrontation. Just a calm resignation letter citing "new opportunities."

Diane acted shocked. Told me I was making a mistake. Said she'd been planning to recommend me for a promotion. (Sure, Diane. Sure you were.)

I walked away from that job with nothing but fifteen months of stolen ideas and blocked opportunities.

But I also walked away with something invaluable.

The Asset Audit From Surviving Diane:

What I gained from that nightmare: the ability to spot career sabotage early. Now I know the red flags. A boss who praises you publicly but never advocates for you privately? Flag. A boss who takes credit for your ideas? Flag. A boss who blocks your advancement while claiming to mentor you? Massive flag.

I also learned that some people see talent as a threat instead of an asset. And working for someone like that—no matter how good the company or the title—is career suicide.

But the biggest lesson? Documentation matters. After Diane, I started keeping records of everything. Ideas I pitched (with dates and emails). Projects I completed (with proof of my contributions). Conversations about advancement (summarized in follow-up emails).

Because if someone's going to sabotage you, they can't do it if you have a paper trail proving your value.

And if they try? You have evidence to take to HR, to skip-level managers, or to your next employer who asks why you left.

* * *

Why Social Toxicity Is Harder to Spot (And What to Do About It)

Here's why Marcus and Diane got away with their bullshit for so long:

Social toxicity is invisible to outsiders.

When your dad criticizes you, people can see it. When your partner monitors your phone, there's evidence. When a family member insults you at Thanksgiving, there are witnesses.

But when a friend systematically diminishes you with "jokes"? That's subjective. "You're too sensitive." "He's just busting your balls." "That's how guys are with each other."

When a boss sabotages you while praising you? That's invisible. Nobody sees the blocked opportunities, the stolen ideas, the private undermining. They just see the glowing performance reviews.

So you start questioning yourself. "Maybe I am too sensitive." "Maybe I'm imagining things." "Maybe I'm the problem."

And that's exactly what toxic people count on.

So here's how to know if you're dealing with social toxicity or just normal relationship friction:

Test #1: The Reciprocity Check

Healthy friendships are roughly balanced. You initiate sometimes, they initiate sometimes. You listen to their problems, they listen to yours. You celebrate their wins, they celebrate yours.

Toxic friendships are one-sided. You're always the one reaching out. Always the one listening. Always the one celebrating while they diminish.

Do the test: stop initiating for a month. If they don't notice, you're not friends—you're their unpaid therapist.

Test #2: The Energy Audit

After you spend time with this person, do you feel better or worse?

Healthy relationships leave you energized (or at least neutral). Toxic relationships leave you drained, anxious, or questioning yourself.

If you consistently feel worse after seeing someone—even if you can't articulate why—trust that feeling. Your nervous system knows what your brain is rationalizing away.

Test #3: The Celebration Check

Think about the last time you had good news. A promotion, an accomplishment, something you were excited about.

How did this person respond?

Real friends celebrate. Toxic people diminish ("That's cool, but..."), redirect ("Oh that reminds me of when I..."), or minimize ("Must be nice to have connections").

If you can't remember the last time they were genuinely happy for you, that's not a friend. That's a competitor in disguise.

Test #4: The Documentation Test (For Work)

If your boss or colleague's public persona doesn't match their private behavior, start documenting everything.

Ideas you pitch (emails with timestamps). Projects you complete (saved files with your name on them). Promises they make (follow-up emails summarizing conversations). Feedback that contradicts their public praise (documented inconsistencies).

If you're not crazy—if the sabotage is real—documentation will prove it. And if you are imagining things, the documentation will show that too.

Either way, you'll have clarity.

* * *

## How to Exit Toxic Social Relationships (Without Drama)

With family, you sometimes have to maintain relationships for practical reasons. With romantic partners, breakups are clear-cut events.

But with friends and coworkers? The exit is murkier.

Here's how to do it:

### For Toxic Friendships: The Slow Fade

You don't need to have a dramatic friend breakup conversation. Just... stop showing up.

Stop initiating plans. Stop responding to texts immediately (or at all). Stop being available for their emotional dumps. Stop pretending you care about their problems when they never cared about yours.

If they notice and ask what's wrong, you can be honest ("I realized this friendship isn't serving me anymore") or diplomatic ("I've been really busy, just prioritizing differently right now"). But chances are? They won't notice. Because they were never really your friend to begin with.

### For Toxic Coworkers: Strategic Distance

You can't always quit your job (bills exist). So you create professional boundaries. Keep interactions brief and documented. Stop sharing ideas in private meetings—pitch them in group settings with witnesses. Stop seeking their approval or mentorship—find advocates elsewhere.

Be polite but distant. Cordial but unavailable. Professional but protective.

And start job searching. Because life's too short to work for people who sabotage you.

For Toxic Bosses: Document, Escalate, Exit

First, document everything (we covered this). Then, if you have a functional HR department or skip-level manager, escalate with evidence. Sometimes organizations will intervene. Sometimes they'll protect the toxic boss because they're "too valuable."

Either way, start looking for new opportunities. And when you leave, be honest in your exit interview. Not vindictive—just factual. "I'm leaving because my manager blocked advancement opportunities while publicly claiming to support my growth." Then provide documentation.

Will it change anything? Maybe not. But it'll be on record for the next person they sabotage.

Social toxicity—bad friends, sabotaging coworkers, undermining bosses—is harder to spot than family toxicity because it hides behind professionalism and shared history. But it's just as damaging. Maybe more so, because you spend more waking hours with these people than you do with your family. So do the tests.

Check for reciprocity. Audit your energy. Notice who celebrates and who diminishes.

And then—without guilt, without drama, without apology—remove the people who drain you. You're allowed to outgrow friendships. You're allowed to leave jobs that don't value you. You're allowed to prioritize your well-being over other people's comfort.

Not selfish. Necessary. Because the alternative is spending your life performing for people who will never applaud. Exit the stage. Find a better audience.

# Chapter 8 Why Failure Is Your Fast Pass: How to Stop Fearing the Best Teacher You'll Ever Have

I bombed a presentation in front of 200 people once.

Not "had a rough moment" bombed. Not "stumbled over a few words" bombed. I mean full-scale, forget-what-slide-I'm-on, lose-my-train-of-thought, watch-people-check-their-phones-while-I'm-talking bombed.

It was a corporate training on leadership—my specialty, something I'd taught dozens of times before. But this audience was different. Senior executives from a Fortune 500 company. High stakes. High expectations. And I completely choked.

About twenty minutes in, I realized I'd lost them. You know that moment when you can feel the energy drain from a room? When you're talking but nobody's actually listening anymore? That was minute twenty.

I had another ninety minutes to go.

I tried to recover. Cracked a joke that landed with silence. Asked an interactive question that got one half-hearted response. Skipped ahead to what I thought was my strongest material, but by then it didn't matter—I'd already lost their trust.

When it finally ended, the polite applause was somehow worse than no applause would have been. A few people thanked me on their way out—the kind of thanks that sounds like sympathy. Most just left.

The client contact pulled me aside afterward. "That wasn't what we expected. We're going to need to discuss whether we'll continue with the remaining sessions."

Translation: You're probably fired.

I drove home in complete silence. Didn't turn on music. Didn't call anyone. Just sat with the weight of having spectacularly failed at something I was supposed to be good at.

And here's what my brain did for the next 48 hours:

Replayed every cringe-worthy moment in high definition. Catastrophized about losing the client, my reputation, future opportunities. Questioned whether I was actually good at this or had just been lucky until now. Considered whether I should quit training altogether and go work at a hardware store where nobody would judge me.

That's Path One. Pure, unfiltered reaction.

* * *

## What Failure Actually Is (When You Stop Catastrophizing)

After two days of self-flagellation, I did something different. I made myself sit down and answer one question:

What did this failure teach me that success never could?

And once I got past the immediate shame, the answers started coming:

**Lesson #1:** I'd been coasting on material that worked for mid-level managers but wasn't calibrated for executives.

Senior executives don't want theory—they want immediate application. They don't want long stories—they want frameworks they can deploy tomorrow. I'd been teaching the same way to every audience, and it worked until it didn't.

That failure forced me to completely rebuild my executive training approach. And the weird thing? That rebuilt approach became my most requested offering.

**Lesson #2:** I'd been winging the first 20 minutes instead of scripting them tight.

I thought I knew my material well enough to improvise the opening. And with most audiences, that worked. But with high-stakes audiences, you need a rock-solid opening that hooks them immediately. I'd been gambling on charisma instead of structure.

After that bomb, I started scripting and practicing my first twenty minutes word-for-word. Made them bulletproof. And I never lost an audience in the opening again.

**Lesson #3:** I had no recovery plan for when things went wrong.

When I lost them at minute twenty, I panicked. I had no protocol for "audience is checked out—how do I re-engage?" So, I just kept plowing forward, hoping it would get better. It didn't.

That failure taught me to build circuit breakers into my presentations—specific moments where I pause, check engagement, and have a backup plan if things aren't landing. Now if I'm losing people, I have tools to course-correct instead of watching the ship sink.

**So, here's what that catastrophic failure gave me:**

A complete redesign of my executive training that made it 10x more effective. A rock-solid opening structure that hooks audiences immediately. And a recovery protocol that prevents small problems from becoming total disasters.

Those three improvements made me thousands of dollars and saved me from countless future failures.

Would I have learned those lessons if the presentation had gone well?

Absolutely not.

Success teaches you what works. Failure teaches you why it works—and that's way more valuable.

* * *

The Failure That Changed My Career (For Real This Time)

Want to hear about an even bigger failure?

I got passed over for a promotion I was absolutely sure I'd get.

This was at my second corporate job, before I went full-time into consulting. I'd been working toward this Director-level position for two years. Done everything right—exceeded performance metrics, took on extra projects, mentored junior staff, made myself indispensable.

When the position opened up, my boss told me I was the frontrunner. HR told me my application was strong. I started planning what I'd do with the salary bump.

And then they gave it to someone else.

Not someone more qualified. Not someone who'd been there longer. Someone who had connections I didn't have. Someone who played politics better than I did.

I was devastated. Not just disappointed—actually devastated. I'd invested two years of my life positioning myself for this role, and it got handed to someone else because of who they knew, not what they could do.

My immediate reaction was pure Path One: rage, resentment, fantasies about quitting dramatically. Then Path Two kicked in: "I guess this is just how corporate works. Maybe I should just accept that I'm not the political type and stay in my lane."

But then something clicked.

I asked myself: What's true about this situation that I don't want to admit?

And the uncomfortable truth was this:

I'd been increasingly frustrated at this company for over a year. I'd been fantasizing about starting my own thing but using "job security" as an excuse not to try. I'd been staying because the promotion dangled the promise of more money and a better title—not because I actually wanted to be there.

If I'd gotten that promotion, I probably would have stayed another five years in a role that was slowly suffocating me.

The reframe:

The reframe: They just freed me. They made the decision I was too scared to make for myself.

Six months later, I'd transitioned into consulting and instructional design work I actually loved. A year after that, I was making more money with more freedom than that promotion would have ever given me.

Did getting passed over still sting? Absolutely. But the reframe turned the sting into fuel. It converted "this is happening TO me" into "this is happening FOR me."

The Asset Audit From That Rejection:

What I gained: permission to leave a situation I'd been too scared to quit. Clarity that I didn't actually want to climb the corporate ladder—I wanted to build my own thing. And proof that sometimes the best thing that can happen to you is not getting what you thought you wanted.

That "failure" wasn't a failure at all. It was a course correction.

* * *

Why We Fear Failure (And Why That Fear Is Bullshit)

Here's the real reason people avoid failure:

They think failure says something permanent about who they are.

If I fail at this business, it means I'm not an entrepreneur.

If I fail at this relationship, it means I'm unlovable.

If I fail at this presentation, it means I'm incompetent.

We've turned failure into identity. And when failure becomes identity, of course you're going to avoid it at all costs.

But here's what failure actually means:

You tried something. It didn't work. Now you have information you didn't have before.

That's it. That's the whole thing.

Failure isn't a verdict on your worth. It's data about what works and what doesn't.

Thomas Edison tried thousands of materials before finding one that worked for the light bulb filament. When someone asked him about all those failures, he said, "I didn't fail. I just found 10,000 ways that won't work."

That's not toxic positivity. That's accurate framing.

Every "failed" attempt eliminated a possibility and narrowed the search space. Every "failure" was actually progress toward the solution.

Same with your failures.

That relationship that didn't work? It taught you what you actually need in a partner.

That business that failed? It taught you what markets won't support and what skills you need to develop.

That presentation that bombed? It taught you what audiences respond to and what makes them check out.

None of those are verdicts on your identity. They're expensive lessons in the school of competence.

And expensive lessons are still lessons.

* * *

The Failure Reframe Framework (How to Extract Value From Any Disaster)

Okay, so you failed at something. Now what?

Here's the system I use to turn failures into assets:

Step One: Feel the feeling (but set a timer)

When you fail, you're going to feel like shit. That's normal. Don't try to skip past it with toxic positivity.

Give yourself permission to be disappointed, angry, embarrassed—whatever the feeling is. But set a time limit. 24 hours. 48 hours. A week if it's a big failure.

Feel the feeling. Process it. And then—when the timer goes off—move to Step Two.

Step Two: Ask the extraction questions

Once you've processed the emotional hit, it's time to extract the lessons. Here are the questions I ask:

What specifically went wrong? (Not "everything"—be specific.)

What was within my control? (Focus here—this is where you have leverage.)

What was outside my control? (Acknowledge this, then let it go.)

What did this teach me that I wouldn't have learned otherwise?

What will I do differently next time? (Be specific—vague commitments don't change behavior.)

Write down the answers. Don't just think about them—actually write them. There's something about externalizing the lessons that makes them stick.

Step Three: Build the improvement

This is the step most people skip. They extract the lessons, feel better about the failure, and then... do nothing with the information.

Don't do that.

Take the lessons from Step Two and turn them into concrete changes. Not "I'll be more prepared next time." That's too vague. Instead: "I will script and practice the first 20 minutes of every high-stakes presentation."

Not "I'll be more careful choosing partners." Instead: "I will not enter a serious relationship with someone who doesn't celebrate my wins."

Not "I'll do better market research next time." Instead: "I will talk to 20 potential customers before building anything."

Specific changes. Behavioral changes. Things you can actually implement.

Step Four: Test the improvement

Here's how you know if the lesson actually stuck: you get another chance to fail, and this time you don't make the same mistake.

You might make a different mistake—that's fine, that's progress. But if you make the same mistake twice, you didn't actually learn the lesson. You just felt temporarily bad about it.

So test it. Put yourself in similar situations. See if the improvement holds.

And if it doesn't? Go back to Step Two and dig deeper.

* * *

Why Failure Is Actually a Fast Pass (Not Just a Platitude)

Here's the uncomfortable truth about success:

You can't get there without failing. Multiple times. Publicly.

Look at anyone who's actually good at something—not lucky, not connected, but genuinely competent—and you'll find a graveyard of failures behind them.

The entrepreneur who built a successful company? They probably killed three businesses before that one took off.

The author with bestselling books? They probably got rejected by 50 agents before someone said yes.

The executive who runs a department? They probably got passed over for promotions, made terrible hiring decisions, and led projects that crashed before they figured it out.

Failure isn't the opposite of success. It's the admission price.

And here's the thing: you can pay that price early and often, learning fast and iterating quickly. Or you can try to avoid failure, which just means you pay the price later—when the stakes are higher and the cost is bigger.

The people who succeed fastest aren't the ones who never fail. They're the ones who fail early, extract the lessons, and don't make the same mistake twice.

That's why failure is a fast pass. It's not a detour—it's the direct route.

Every failure eliminates a path that doesn't work. Every failure teaches you something success can't. Every failure makes you slightly better at spotting problems before they become disasters.

So stop fearing failure. Start collecting it.

I bombed that presentation seven years ago. I got passed over for that promotion nine years ago.

Both felt like the end of the world at the time.

But today, I run a successful training business built on the lessons those failures taught me. I make more money and have more freedom than any corporate promotion would have given me. And I genuinely can't imagine my career without those "disasters."

Because they weren't disasters. They were course corrections disguised as setbacks.

Your failures are the same.

So fail. Fail spectacularly if possible. Fail early and often. Extract the lessons. Build the improvements. And watch how fast you get where you're actually supposed to be.

Because success isn't about avoiding failure. It's about failing better.

# Chapter 9 The Gratitude Flip: Why Most Gratitude Advice Is Toxic Positivity in Disguise

I tried keeping a gratitude journal once.

This was about ten years ago, during one of those phases where I was convinced I just needed the right productivity hack to fix my life. Every self-help book, every motivational podcast, every Instagram therapist was preaching gratitude like it was the secret to happiness.

"Just write down three things you're grateful for every day! It rewires your brain! It'll change your life!"

So I bought a nice journal. Set a reminder on my phone. Committed to doing it every morning.

Day one: "I'm grateful for my health, my family, and my job."

Day two: "I'm grateful for coffee, my home, and my friends."

Day three: "I'm grateful for... uh... sunshine? My car? The fact that I'm not actively dying?"

By day seven, I was phoning it in. "I'm grateful for air conditioning, WiFi, and the invention of pants."

By day fourteen, I'd stopped entirely.

Not because I wasn't grateful—I was. But the exercise felt performative. Like I was checking a box to prove to myself that I was doing personal development correctly. "See? I wrote down three things! I'm growing as a person!"

Except I didn't feel any different. I wasn't happier. I wasn't more present. I was just someone who'd wasted $20 on a journal I'd never finish.

And I thought: maybe gratitude is overrated. Maybe it's just another self-help scam designed to make you feel inadequate if you're not sufficiently thankful for your mediocre life.

Turns out, I was half right.

* * *

## Why Most Gratitude Advice Is Actually Toxic Positivity

Here's the problem with the way gratitude gets taught:

It's almost always framed as "just appreciate what you have instead of wanting more." Which sounds reasonable until you realize what that actually means in practice:

Shut up about your problems. Other people have it worse.

That's not gratitude. That's guilt disguised as wisdom.

You're struggling financially? Well, be grateful you're not homeless.

You're miserable in your relationship? Be grateful you're not alone.

You're burned out at work? Be grateful you have a job.

This version of gratitude isn't about appreciation—it's about suppression. It's about making you feel bad for wanting your life to be better. It's the "At Least" reflex weaponized as personal development.

And that's why gratitude journals fail for most people. Because when you sit down to write "I'm grateful for my job," but you actually hate your job, you're not practicing gratitude. You're practicing denial.

Real gratitude doesn't require you to pretend your problems don't exist. Real gratitude coexists with wanting things to be better.

You can be grateful for your job and be actively looking for a better one.

You can appreciate your current relationship and acknowledge it needs work.

You can be thankful for your health and still be dealing with chronic pain.

Both things can be true. That's the actual practice.

* * *

What Actually Changed My Mind About Gratitude

About two years after I abandoned the gratitude journal, something happened that made me reconsider the whole thing.

My mom had her stroke. (You read about this in Chapter 5.) And in the aftermath—during those first few weeks when we didn't know if she'd recover, when every day felt like waiting for the next disaster—I found myself doing something weird.

Every morning when I woke up, before I checked my phone or got out of bed, I'd run through a mental inventory:

My mom was still alive.

Izzy is healthy.

I woke up today, which means I get another shot at being useful.

That's it. Three things. But not the generic "I'm grateful for family" nonsense from my abandoned journal. These were specific, urgent, true-in-this-moment observations.

And here's what I noticed: doing this didn't make the stress go away. It didn't fix anything. My mom was still declining. The uncertainty was still crushing.

But it gave me about thirty seconds of clarity before the panic set in. Thirty seconds where I remembered that despite everything falling apart, some things were still holding.

That's when I understood what gratitude actually does.

It doesn't erase your problems. It doesn't make you stop wanting things to be better. It just reminds your brain—which is catastrophizing about everything that could go wrong—that some things are still okay.

It's an anchor. Not a cure.

* * *

What Gratitude Actually Does to Your Brain (The Non-Bullshit Version)

Okay, brief detour into neuroscience because it's actually relevant here.

Your brain has a negativity bias. We covered this in Chapter 2, but here's the reminder: your brain is wired to scan for threats. It's constantly running worst-case scenarios, looking for problems, catastrophizing about what could go wrong.

This kept your ancestors alive when threats were things like "Is that rustling in the bushes a tiger?" But it makes you miserable in modern life when the threats are mostly imaginary.

Your brain is so good at finding problems that it will actively ignore good things to focus on potential disasters. You could have 99 things going well and one thing going badly, and your brain will spend 90% of its energy obsessing over the bad thing.

This is where gratitude comes in.

Gratitude isn't magic. It's deliberate attention redirection. It's you manually overriding your brain's default threat-scanning mode and forcing it to acknowledge what's actually working.

Think of it like this: your brain is a search engine. Whatever you tell it to search for, it'll find. If you tell it to search for problems, it'll find infinite problems. If you tell it to search for things that are okay, it'll find those too.

Gratitude is just you deciding what you're searching for.

And here's the kicker: the more you practice directing your attention toward what's working, the better your brain gets at noticing those things automatically. It's like training a muscle. At first, it's hard and unnatural. But eventually, your brain starts defaulting to "what's okay" instead of "what's catastrophic."

That's not toxic positivity. That's just how neuroplasticity works.

* * *

## The Gratitude Practice That Actually Works (No Journal Required)

Okay, so if gratitude journals are performative bullshit, what actually works?

Here's what I do now. It's stupidly simple, which is probably why it works.

### The Morning Anchor (30 Seconds, That's It)

Every morning, before I get out of bed, I do the mental inventory. Three specific things that are true right now. Not generic "I'm grateful for my health" nonsense. Specific, urgent, this-matters-today observations.

Some days it's: "Izzy didn't have a seizure last night. I have work that matters. Coffee exists."

Some days it's: "I'm not in physical pain right now. Nobody I love died yesterday. I get to try again today."

The specificity matters. Generic gratitude doesn't stick. Specific gratitude does.

The Crisis Interrupt (When Your Brain Is Spiraling)

When I catch myself catastrophizing—when my brain is running the "everything is falling apart" program—I force myself to name three things that are still okay.

Not three things I'm grateful for. Not three silver linings. Just three factual observations about what hasn't collapsed yet.

"I'm stressed about money. But I'm not homeless. I'm not starving. I still have options."

"Work is a disaster. But I'm not fired yet. I have skills. I could find another job if I had to."

This isn't denial. It's calibration. It's reminding my brain that even though things are bad, they're not apocalyptic.

The Micro-Moment Practice (Throughout the Day)

This is the hardest one because it requires being present, which nobody is anymore.

When something genuinely good happens—even something tiny—I pause for five seconds and actually notice it.

Izzy laughs at something I said. I pause. Notice the sound. Notice that we're still connected after all these years. Notice that this moment exists.

The first sip of coffee hits exactly right. I pause. Notice the taste. Notice that I'm alert enough to appreciate it. Notice that this is a good thirty seconds.

My nephew texts me something funny. I pause. Notice that I have people who think of me. Notice that connection still matters. Notice that this made me smile.

Five seconds. That's it. Just long enough to register that something good happened instead of scrolling past it to the next crisis.

You do this enough times, and your brain starts automatically flagging good moments instead of only bad ones.

* * *

Why This Isn't the Same as Toxic Positivity (And Why That Matters)

Here's how you know if you're doing real gratitude versus toxic positivity:

Toxic positivity says: "Don't be sad. Look on the bright side!"

Real gratitude says: "You're allowed to be sad. And also, some things are still okay."

Toxic positivity requires you to pretend problems don't exist.

Real gratitude acknowledges problems and then looks for what's still functioning despite them.

Toxic positivity is performative—it's about proving you're sufficiently grateful.

Real gratitude is pragmatic—it's about training your brain to notice what's working so you don't spiral into hopelessness.

When my mom was dying, toxic positivity would have been: "At least she lived a long life! Be grateful for the time you had!"

Real gratitude was: "This is devastating. And also, she's still here today. I can still talk to her. That matters."

See the difference?

One dismisses your pain. The other holds your pain and your appreciation at the same time.

That's the practice. Not pretending everything is fine. But noticing what's still standing while everything else burns.

* * *

What Actually Changed When I Started Doing This

I've been doing some version of this practice for about five years now. Not perfectly. Not every single day. But consistently enough that it's become automatic.

And here's what's different:

I'm not happier. That's not what this does. Bad things still happen. Stress still exists. I still have days where everything feels like it's falling apart.

But I'm more stable. When something goes wrong now, I don't immediately spiral into "everything is terrible and will always be terrible." My brain has been trained to automatically look for what's still okay. It's like having a built-in circuit breaker for catastrophizing. I notice good moments more. Not because I'm more optimistic—I'm not. But because I've trained myself to actually register them instead of scrolling past.

And weirdly, I'm more honest about when things suck. Because I'm not trying to force gratitude as a way to avoid acknowledging problems. I can say "this is terrible" without my brain immediately adding "but I should be grateful anyway." That's the paradox: real gratitude makes you more honest about your problems, not less. Because you're not using appreciation as a weapon against yourself. So forget the gratitude journal. Forget the Instagram platitudes about how blessed you are. Forget the guilt trips about people who have it worse.

Just do this:

Every morning, name three specific things that are okay right now. When you're spiraling, pause and name three things that haven't collapsed yet. When something genuinely good happens, pause for five seconds and actually notice it. That's it. No journal. No performance. No pretending your problems don't exist.

Just training your brain to notice what's working alongside what isn't. Because both things can be true. And that's the whole point.

# Chapter 10 The Stoic Secret: How Ancient Romans Figured Out Emotional Control Better Than Modern Therapy

I discovered Stoicism the way most people do: by accident, during a crisis, when nothing else was working.

This was about eight years ago. I was dealing with a work situation that was eating me alive—a client who kept moving the goalposts, demanding more work for the same pay, and threatening to leave bad reviews if I didn't comply.

I was furious. Not just annoyed—actively, constantly furious. I'd wake up thinking about it. I'd go to bed replaying conversations. I'd spend hours mentally composing emails I'd never send. The situation was consuming me.

And then a friend recommended a book: "Meditations" by Marcus Aurelius. Said it helped him deal with stress. I was skeptical—what could a Roman emperor from 2,000 years ago teach me about dealing with difficult clients?

Turns out: everything.

The book is basically Marcus Aurelius writing journal entries to himself about how to deal with people who annoyed him, situations he couldn't control, and his own emotional reactions. And right there on page one was this line that stopped me cold:

"You have power over your mind—not outside events. Realize this, and you will find strength."

And I realized: I'd been spending all my energy trying to control the client. Trying to make him be reasonable. Trying to make him stop being difficult. Trying to change external circumstances.

Which was completely futile. Because I couldn't control him. I could only control how I responded.

That realization—that simple, ancient realization—changed everything.

* * *

What Stoicism Actually Is (Not the Emotionless Robot Thing)

Here's what most people get wrong about Stoicism:

They think it means being emotionless. Suppressing feelings. Never getting upset. Being a robot who doesn't care about anything.

That's not Stoicism. That's repression with a philosophy degree.

Real Stoicism is about recognizing what you can control and what you can't—and then putting all your energy into the first category while accepting the second.

It's not "don't feel your feelings." It's "feel your feelings, but don't let them control your actions."

Here's the core idea in the simplest terms possible:

Some things are up to you. Most things aren't. Focus on the first category. Accept the second.

That's it. That's the whole philosophy.

What's up to you: your thoughts, your actions, your reactions, your judgments, your effort.

What's not up to you: other people's behavior, external events, outcomes, what people think of you, the past, the future.

And the Stoics figured out—2,000 years before modern psychology caught up—that most human suffering comes from trying to control the second category.

You're miserable because you're trying to control things that are fundamentally uncontrollable. And the harder you try, the more powerless you feel.

The Stoic solution? Stop trying. Redirect that energy to what you actually can control.

* * *

How I Actually Applied This to the Nightmare Client

Back to my difficult client situation.

After reading Marcus Aurelius, I did something I'd never done before: I made two lists.

List One: Things I Cannot Control

Whether this client is reasonable. Whether he appreciates my work. Whether he leaves a bad review. Whether he decides to pay me fairly. Whether he respects my boundaries. How he treats me in emails.

List Two: Things I CAN Control

Whether I continue working with him. How I respond to his emails. What boundaries I set. Whether I let his behavior consume my mental energy. How much work I agree to do. Whether I walk away.

And once I saw it written out like that, the path forward was obvious.

I'd been wasting all my energy on List One—trying to make him be different, hoping he'd suddenly become reasonable, catastrophizing about bad reviews. None of which I could control.

Meanwhile, I'd been ignoring List Two—the things I actually had power over.

So I made a decision. I sent one final email:

"I've completed the work we originally agreed to. If you need additional work, here's my rate for that. If that doesn't work for you, no hard feelings—I'll close out the project here."

That's it. No justification. No emotional explanation. Just clarity about what I was willing to do and what I wasn't.

He responded with a long, angry email about how unprofessional I was being. (List One: not my problem.) He threatened a bad review. (List One: still not my problem.) He demanded I complete the additional work "as part of the original agreement." (List One: nope, still can't control him.)

And I didn't respond. I closed the project. Refunded a prorated amount to be fair. And moved on.

Did he leave a bad review? Yep. (List One.) Did it hurt my business? Not even a little. (Because I'd stopped catastrophizing about it, which was List Two.)

And here's what changed:

The anger disappeared immediately. Not because I'd suppressed it—because I'd stopped trying to control something I couldn't control. The moment I accepted that I couldn't make him be reasonable, the fury evaporated.

That's the Stoic secret. Most of your emotional suffering comes from trying to control things you can't control. Stop trying, and the suffering stops too.

* * *

The Dichotomy of Control (Or: How to Know What to Let Go)

The Stoics had a fancy name for this concept: the Dichotomy of Control. Which sounds more complicated than it is.

Here's how to apply it to literally any situation that's stressing you out:

Step One: Identify the situation that's causing stress.

Be specific. "I'm stressed about work" is too vague. "I'm stressed because my boss might pass me over for a promotion" is specific.

Step Two: Make the two lists.

List One: What can't I control about this situation?

List Two: What CAN I control?

Be ruthlessly honest here. Most people put things in List Two that actually belong in List One because they don't want to admit they're powerless.

Step Three: Accept everything on List One.

This is the hard part. Accepting doesn't mean liking. It doesn't mean approval. It just means acknowledging reality: you cannot control this thing, so fighting it is pointless.

You can't control whether your boss gives you the promotion. You can't control whether the company goes through layoffs. You can't control the economy. You can't control other candidates' qualifications.

Fighting any of those things is wasted energy.

Step Four: Focus all your energy on List Two.

This is where your power lives. You can control the quality of your work. You can control how you present yourself. You can control whether you network with decision-makers. You can control whether you document your achievements. You can control your backup plan if the promotion doesn't happen.

All of that is List Two. All of that is yours.

And here's what happens when you do this consistently:

You stop catastrophizing. Because catastrophizing is imagining all the terrible things that might happen in List One—the category you can't control. Once you accept that category, there's nothing left to catastrophize about.

You become more effective. Because all your energy is going toward things you can actually change instead of being wasted on resentment, worry, and magical thinking.

You feel more powerful. Not because you're controlling more—because you're focused on what you actually can control.

* * *

The Traffic Example (Or: Why Road Rage Is Just Bad Philosophy)

Let me give you the most mundane, relatable example of Stoicism in action: traffic.

You're driving to an important meeting. You leave early to account for traffic. And then—because the universe has a sense of humor—there's an accident on the highway. Complete standstill. You're going to be late.

Here's what most people do:

Get angry. Honk the horn (even though that accomplishes nothing). Curse at other drivers. Catastrophize about the meeting. Check the GPS obsessively hoping for a miracle. Call ahead to explain why you'll be late (while still stressed about it). Spend the entire drive furious and helpless.

All of that is trying to control List One: the traffic, the accident, the time.

Here's the Stoic approach:

Acknowledge that you cannot control the traffic. You cannot make the accident un-happen. You cannot make time move faster. (List One: accepted.)

Then focus on what you CAN control: You can call ahead calmly and reschedule. You can use the time to listen to a podcast or audiobook. You can practice being present instead of catastrophizing. You can choose not to let this ruin your entire day. (List Two: engaged.)

Same situation. Completely different experience.

One version leaves you stressed, angry, and powerless. The other leaves you calm, productive, and in control of your response.

That's not because the Stoic is somehow better at suppressing emotions. It's because they've correctly identified what's worth their energy and what isn't.

Road rage is just bad philosophy. It's getting angry at List One.

* * *

The Hard Part About Stoicism (That Nobody Warns You About)

Here's what nobody tells you about practicing Stoicism:

Most of the things you care about are in List One.

Whether your kids turn out okay? List One. You can influence them, but you can't control their choices.

Whether your partner stays with you? List One. You can be a good partner, but you can't control their feelings or decisions.

Whether your business succeeds? List One. You can work hard and make good decisions, but you can't control the market, competitors, or luck.

Whether people like you? List One. You can be likable, but you can't control their preferences or judgments.

This is brutal to accept. Because it means most of what you desperately want to control is fundamentally outside your control.

And this is where people misunderstand Stoicism and think it means "don't care about anything."

But that's not what it means.

You're allowed to care deeply about your kids. You're allowed to want your business to succeed. You're allowed to hope your partner stays with you.

What you're not allowed to do—if you want to maintain your sanity—is attach your happiness to those outcomes.

Because if your happiness depends on things you can't control, you've made yourself permanently vulnerable to circumstances.

The Stoic solution: Care about the outcome. Hope for the outcome. Work toward the outcome. But base your peace of mind on whether you did everything in your power (List Two), not on whether you got the result you wanted (List One).

You can be devastated if your business fails. That's human. But you shouldn't be ashamed if you gave it everything you had.

You can grieve if your relationship ends. That's natural. But you shouldn't beat yourself up if you did your best to be a good partner.

You can worry about your kids. That's part of being a parent. But you shouldn't torture yourself over their choices once they're adults.

That's the practice. Control what you can. Accept what you can't. And find peace in the distinction.

* * *

## What Changed After Eight Years of This Practice

I've been practicing some version of Stoicism for eight years now. Not perfectly—I still get angry at things I can't control. I still catastrophize sometimes. I still waste energy on List One.

But I catch myself faster now. When I start spiraling about something, I automatically ask: "Is this List One or List Two?"

If it's List One, I redirect. If it's List Two, I engage.

And here's what's different:

I'm less angry. Not because I've suppressed my anger—because I've stopped directing it at things I can't change.

I'm more effective. Because all my problem-solving energy goes toward actual solutions instead of being wasted on resentment.

I'm less anxious. Because most anxiety comes from trying to control the future, which is the ultimate List One category.

I'm better at letting go. Not because I don't care—because I've accepted that caring deeply about something doesn't mean I can control it.

And weirdly, I'm more ambitious. Because when you stop wasting energy fighting reality, you have a lot more energy to build the things you actually want.

So here's the Stoic secret in one sentence:

Most of your suffering comes from trying to control things you can't control. Stop trying, and the suffering stops too.

That's it. That's the whole thing.

Make your two lists. Accept List One. Focus on List Two.

It won't make you emotionless. It won't make you stop caring. It won't erase your problems.

But it will make you more powerful. Because you'll stop wasting energy on things that were never yours to control.

And that's as close to peace as any of us are going to get.

# Chapter 11: The Stress Field Guide—How to Stay Sane When Specific Things Go Wrong

You know how most stress advice is weirdly generic? "Just breathe." "Stay positive." "Focus on what you can control." Cool. Super helpful when your bank account is in the negatives, your in-laws are passive-aggressively destroying Thanksgiving, and you have a presentation in three hours that could make or break your career.

Here's the problem with generic stress advice:

Different stressors need different strategies. The technique that works when you're worried about money does NOT work when you're dealing with a toxic coworker. The mindset that helps you handle social anxiety will NOT help you perform under a deadline. So today? We're getting specific.

This isn't theory. This is a field guide for the three stress types that ruin most people's happiness:

1. Financial Stress — When money problems keep you up at night
2. Social Stress — When other people are the problem

3. Performance Stress — When you have to deliver under pressure

By the end of this chapter, you'll know exactly which tool to use for which situation. Because stress is manageable—once you stop treating all stress like it's the same thing.

**Part A: Financial Stress — How to Stop Money From Stealing Your Peace**

Let's start with the big one. The stress that wakes you up at 3 AM. The stress that makes you check your bank account seventeen times a day like the number might magically change. The stress that turns every unexpected expense into a full-blown existential crisis. Financial stress. And if you've ever experienced it (spoiler: you have), you know it hits different than other kinds of stress. Because money stress doesn't just live in your head—it lives in your BODY.

It's the knot in your stomach when a bill arrives. It's the panic when your card gets declined. It's the shame spiral when you compare your financial situation to people who seem to have it all figured out. So let's talk about how to handle it without losing your mind.

**Why Financial Stress Feels Uniquely Awful**

Financial stress is brutal because it hits you on multiple levels:

1. It feels like survival. Your lizard brain doesn't understand the difference between "I might lose my house" and "I might get eaten by a tiger." Both trigger the same panic response. 2. It feels never-ending.

Other problems have finish lines. Financial stress? That just keeps showing up, month after month, bill after bill.

3. It feels shameful. Society treats financial struggle like a moral failing. Like if you were smarter, harder-working, or more responsible, you wouldn't be in this situation. (That's garbage, by the way. But it's the message you've internalized, which makes the stress ten times worse.)

So if you're stressed about money right now, first things first:

You're not broken. The system is just really, really hard. And beating yourself up about it? That doesn't help. It just adds emotional stress on top of financial stress.

So let's stop doing that and start fixing this.

**The "Financial Reality Reset" — Get Clear on What You're Actually Dealing With**

Most people avoid looking at their finances when they're stressed. They don't check their bank account. They don't open bills. They just exist in a fog of vague financial dread.

And that? That makes the stress WORSE. Because your brain fills in the blanks with worst-case scenarios. "I'm probably totally screwed." "This is probably way worse than I think." "I'm probably one bill away from complete disaster."

Meanwhile, reality might not be that bad. Or it might be bad, but SPECIFIC bad—which means you can actually DO something about it.

So here's your first move:

**The 10-Minute Financial Reality Check**

Grab a piece of paper (or open a notes app) and write down:

1. How much money do I have RIGHT NOW?
   Not how much you wish you had. Not how much you "should" have. What's actually in the account?

2. What bills are DUE in the next 30 days?
   List them. All of them. Even the ones you're scared to think about.

3. What's the ACTUAL gap between what I have and what I owe?
   This is the number you're dealing with. Not some vague sense of doom—a real, specific number.

Why does this help? Because once you NAME the problem, it stops being a shapeless monster and starts being a solvable math problem. And solvable problems? Those don't keep you up at night.

**The "Future Credit" Mindset — Stop Living Like You're Already Broke**

Here's something weird that happens when you're financially stressed:

You start acting broke BEFORE you actually are. You stop doing anything that costs money—even small things that bring you joy. You cancel plans. You skip social events. You deny yourself every tiny pleasure.

And you tell yourself: "I can't afford to be happy right now."

Which is insane. Because now you're broke AND miserable.

Here's a better approach:

**The $20 Happiness Budget**

Every week, give yourself $20 to spend on something that makes you feel human. Could be:

- Coffee with a friend
- A book you've been wanting
- A meal that isn't ramen
- A small thing that makes you smile

"But I can't afford $20!" Okay, make it $10. Make it $5. Hell, make it $2.

The point isn't the amount. The point is REFUSING to put your entire life on hold just because money is tight. Because if you make happiness contingent on financial security, you'll be miserable until you're rich. And that's not a plan. That's self-imposed torture.

**The "Control What You Can, Let Go of the Rest" Money Rule**

Financial stress loves to spiral because there's so much you CAN'T control. The economy. Inflation. Your company's budget cuts. Unexpected emergencies.

And if you spend all your energy stressing about those? You'll go insane.

So here's the rule:

**Divide your money stress into two categories:**

**Category 1: Things I Can Control**

- How much I spend this week
- Whether I pick up an extra shift
- If I negotiate my next bill
- Whether I start a side hustle
- If I ask for help when I need it

**Category 2: Things I Can't Control**

- The economy
- Gas prices
- Whether I get the raise
- Unexpected emergencies that haven't happened yet

For Category 1? Take action. Make a plan. Do ONE thing today that moves you forward.

For Category 2? Let it go. I know. Easier said than done. But here's the truth: Worrying about things you can't control doesn't prepare you for them. It just drains your energy so you can't handle Category 1 effectively.

So focus on what's in your power. And release the rest.

**The "Worst-Case Scenario" Reality Check**

When you're financially stressed, your brain loves to catastrophize. "If I can't pay this bill, I'll lose my apartment, end up on the street, and die alone under a bridge." Okay. Let's walk that through.

**What's the ACTUAL worst-case scenario?**

Not the movie version. The real one. Let's say you can't pay the bill this month. What ACTUALLY happens?

- Late fee? Probably.
- Phone call? Maybe.
- Eviction after one missed payment? Almost never.

Most worst-case scenarios have steps between "I can't pay" and "complete disaster."

And when you map those out?

You realize: "Okay, this sucks. But it's not the end of the world. And I have options."

And just like that? The panic subsides. Because you're no longer fighting an imaginary apocalypse. You're handling a real problem with real solutions.

**Your Financial Stress Action Plan**

Alright, here's your game plan when money stress hits:

Step 1: Do the 10-Minute Financial Reality Check. Get clear on the actual numbers. Step 2: Identify ONE thing you can do TODAY to improve the situation.

Then do it. Step 3: Protect your $20 Happiness Budget (or whatever amount works). Don't put joy on hold.

Step 4: Catch catastrophic thinking and reality-check it. What's ACTUALLY going to happen?

Step 5: Let go of what you can't control. Seriously. Let. It. Go.

Because financial stress is real. But it doesn't have to steal your entire life. And the moment you stop letting it run the show? You get your peace back—even if the money situation hasn't fully resolved yet.

**Part B: Social Stress — When Other People Are the Problem (And How to Not Let Them Ruin Your Day)**

Alright, let's talk about the stress that doesn't show up on a spreadsheet but still makes you want to fake your own death and move to a remote island. Social stress. The coworker who "just has a quick question" seventeen times a day. The family member who turns every gathering into an emotional hostage situation. The friend who only texts when they need something. The person who somehow makes YOU feel crazy for having boundaries. If you've ever felt your mood tank the second a certain person's name popped up on your phone?

Yeah. That's social stress. And it's insidious because you can't just "solve" it like a math problem. You can't eliminate people from your life without consequences. So you end up stuck—managing relationships that drain you while pretending everything is fine. Let's fix that.

**Why Social Stress is Different (And Why Normal Stress Advice Doesn't Work)**

Social stress isn't about tasks or deadlines. It's about PEOPLE—which means it's messy, emotional, and weirdly personal.

And here's what makes it brutal:

1. You can't control other people.
You can control your calendar, your to-do list, your environment. But you can't control how someone else behaves.

2. You probably care about these people.
If you didn't care, you'd just cut them off. But because they're family, friends, or colleagues, you're stuck trying to maintain the relationship while also protecting your sanity.

3. Setting boundaries feels mean.
Society has convinced you that saying "no" or protecting your energy makes you selfish. So you keep sacrificing your peace to keep others happy.

Which is why so many people stay trapped in draining relationships—and wonder why they're always exhausted. So let's change that.

**The "Not My Circus" Rule — Stop Absorbing Other People's Chaos**

Here's a hard truth:

Other people's problems are not your responsibility. I know. That sounds harsh.

But think about it:

When someone complains to you for the 47th time about the same issue they refuse to fix—is that YOUR problem? When a family member starts drama at dinner—is that YOUR job to fix? When a coworker dumps their stress on you—are you required to carry it? No.

But here's what probably happens:

Someone vents. You absorb their stress. You try to fix it. They don't actually want solutions. They just wanted to complain. And now YOU'RE stressed while THEY feel better.

Sound familiar?

Here's the fix:

**The "Not My Circus, Not My Monkeys" Mantra**

Next time someone tries to drag you into their chaos, mentally repeat:

"Not my circus. Not my monkeys." And then? Don't engage. Examples:

Them: "Oh my God, everything is falling apart."
You: "That sounds stressful. What are you going to do about it?"
(Notice: You didn't offer to solve it. You put it back on them.)

Them: "Can you believe what [person] did?"
You: "Huh. Wild."
(Notice: You didn't take the bait. You just... let it sit there.)

Them: "I need to vent for like an hour."
You: "I've got 10 minutes if you want to talk. After

that, I have to run."
(Notice: You set a time limit. You're not a 24/7 emotional dumping ground.)

This isn't cold. This is self-preservation. Because the moment you stop absorbing everyone else's stress, you get your energy back.

**The "Gray Rock Method" — How to Bore Difficult People Into Leaving You Alone**

Some people thrive on drama. They LOVE getting a reaction out of you. They poke. They prod. They say things designed to get you worked up.

And the more you engage? The more they escalate.

So here's the trick:

Become the most boring person alive. Seriously. This is called the Gray Rock Method, and it's devastatingly effective.

Here's how it works:

When someone tries to bait you:

- Don't argue
- Don't defend yourself
- Don't explain
- Don't justify

Just give bland, boring, one-word responses.

Them: "Wow, you're wearing THAT?"
You: "Yep."

Them: "You know, if you did things MY way..."
You: "Interesting."

Them: "Are you even LISTENING to me?"
You: "Mm-hmm."

No emotion. No reaction. Just gray rock energy.

And guess what happens? They get bored and move on. Because difficult people feed on your reactions. And if you don't give them any? They lose interest.

It's not engaging. It's not satisfying. And eventually, they'll find someone else to bother.

**The "Boundary Statement" — How to Say No Without Apologizing**

Most people suck at boundaries because they apologize while setting them. "I'm so sorry, but I can't help you move this weekend. I know that's terrible of me, and I feel awful, but..." Stop. Boundaries don't require apologies. You're allowed to protect your time, energy, and peace WITHOUT feeling guilty.

Here's how to set a boundary like a boss:

**The Clean No**

"I can't do that." That's it. Full stop.

No explanation. No justification. No "I'm so sorry but..."

Just: "I can't do that."

And if they push? "I understand you're disappointed, but my answer is no." Will they be annoyed? Maybe. Will they respect you more in the long run?

Absolutely. Because people treat you how you teach them to treat you.

And the moment you stop apologizing for having boundaries, they stop testing them.

**The "Energy Audit" — Identify Who's Draining You (And What to Do About It)**

Time for some brutal honesty.

Grab a piece of paper and divide it into two columns:

Column 1: People Who Give Me Energy
These are the people who make you feel GOOD after you interact with them. You leave feeling lighter, happier, energized.

Column 2: People Who Drain My Energy
These are the people who leave you feeling exhausted, frustrated, or stressed. Even when the interaction is "fine," you still feel worse after.

Now look at Column 2. How much time are you spending with those people? And more importantly: WHY?

Because here's the thing:

You're allowed to limit contact with people who drain you—even if they're family. You're allowed to set boundaries with people who exhaust you—even if they're friends. You're allowed to protect your peace—even if it makes other people uncomfortable. And the moment you start prioritizing your energy over other people's expectations? Social stress drops dramatically.

**Your Social Stress Action Plan**

Here's your game plan when people are the problem:

Step 1: Use the "Not My Circus" rule. Stop absorbing other people's chaos. Step 2: Try the Gray Rock Method on difficult people. Bore them into leaving you alone. Step 3: Practice the Clean No. Set boundaries without apologizing.

Step 4: Do an Energy Audit. Identify who drains you and limit exposure.

Step 5: Protect your peace like it's your job. Because it is. Because social stress is optional. Not always easy to eliminate. But absolutely optional. And the moment you stop letting other people steal your happiness? You get it back—immediately.

**Part C: Performance Stress — How to Deliver Under Pressure Without Losing Your Mind**

Alright, final stress type. The big presentation. The important exam. The deadline that matters. The interview that could change everything.

Performance stress. The kind where you're expected to show up, perform flawlessly, and make it look easy—while your brain screams, "WE'RE ALL GONNA DIE."

And here's what makes performance stress uniquely brutal:

It's time-sensitive. You can't just "work on it later." The clock is ticking. The stakes are real. And your brain is very aware that failure is a possibility.

So let's talk about how to handle it like a pro—instead of spiraling into panic mode.

### Why Performance Stress Hits Different

Performance stress is sneaky because it doesn't just make you nervous—it makes you WORSE at the thing you're trying to do. Why?

Because stress floods your brain with cortisol, which:

- Shuts down your prefrontal cortex (the part that thinks clearly)
- Activates your amygdala (the part that screams "DANGER!")
- Makes you overthink, second-guess, and freeze

Which means the MORE stressed you are, the WORSE you perform. It's a vicious cycle. And if you don't know how to break it? You're screwed. So let's fix that.

### The "Pre-Game Ritual" — Train Your Brain to Flip Into Focus Mode

Elite athletes don't just "show up" and hope they perform well. They have a PRE-GAME RITUAL. A specific routine they do before every performance to get their brain in the right state. And guess what? You can do the same thing. Here's how:

### Step 1: Create Your Focus Trigger

Pick a simple action you can do right before you need to perform. Could be:

- Taking three deep breaths
- Listening to a specific song

- Saying a specific phrase ("Let's go" or "I've got this")
- A physical gesture (fist pump, shoulder roll, etc.)

**Step 2: Use It Every Time**

Before every presentation, exam, interview, or high-stakes moment—do the ritual.

Your brain will start associating that action with "time to focus."

And over time? It becomes automatic. You do the ritual. Your brain flips into performance mode. You execute.

**The "Channel the Energy" Technique — Turn Nervous Into Excited**

Here's a weird fact:

Nervousness and excitement feel EXACTLY the same in your body.

Heart racing? Same.
Adrenaline pumping? Same.
Sweaty palms? Same.

The only difference? The story you tell yourself.

So here's the trick:

**Stop saying "I'm nervous."**

**Start saying "I'm excited."**

Out loud. Seriously. Your brain believes what you tell it. And when you label the feeling as "excitement" instead of "anxiety," your performance improves DRAMATICALLY. Studies prove this. It's not just motivational fluff. So next time you feel that pre-performance panic?

Say: "I'm excited. This is going to be great."

And watch how fast your brain shifts gears.

**The "Shrink the Moment" Strategy — Make It Feel Smaller**

Performance stress loves to inflate the stakes.

Your brain says:

- "This is EVERYTHING."
- "If I mess this up, my life is over."
- "Everyone is watching and judging me."

Which makes you freeze.

So here's how to shrink it back down:

**The 5-Year Test**

Ask yourself: "Will this matter in 5 years?"

If the answer is yes? Okay, it matters. Give it your focus.

If the answer is no? Then it's not as big as your brain is making it.

**The "One Person" Focus**

Instead of thinking "I have to impress EVERYONE," pick ONE person. Deliver your presentation like you're talking to that one person. Give your best for that one person. It's way less overwhelming than trying to please a crowd.

**The "I've Done Hard Things Before" Reminder**

Think of a time when you were stressed about something—and you handled it.

Remind yourself: "I've been here before. I survived. I'll survive this too."

Because you've been through harder things than this. And you made it. Which means you'll make it through this too.

**The "Dump the Pressure" Technique — Get It Out of Your Head**

Here's something nobody tells you:

Writing down your stress makes it smaller. Seriously.

If you're spiraling before a big performance, grab a piece of paper and write:

- What are you actually afraid of?
- What's the worst that could realistically happen?
- What's ONE thing you can do right now to prepare?

Just getting it out of your head and onto paper? It immediately feels more manageable. Because now it's external—not swirling around in your brain, getting bigger and scarier.

**Your Performance Stress Action Plan**

Here's your game plan when you have to deliver under pressure:

Step 1: Create a Pre-Game Ritual. Train your brain to flip into focus mode. Step 2: Relabel "nervous" as "excited." Channel the energy. Step 3: Shrink the moment. Use the 5-Year Test or One Person Focus. Step 4: Dump the pressure. Write it down to get it out of your head.

Step 5: Remind yourself: You've handled hard things before. You'll handle this too. Because performance stress is real. But it doesn't have to destroy you. And the moment you learn how to manage it? You stop fearing high-stakes moments—and start showing up as your best self.

**Final Thought: Stress is Manageable When You Know Which Tool to Use**

Look, stress is part of life. Money will be tight sometimes. People will be difficult. You'll have to perform under pressure.

But here's what you now know:

Different stressors need different strategies. And when you know exactly which tool to use for which situation? Stress stops feeling overwhelming and starts feeling manageable.

So next time stress hits, ask yourself:

"Is this financial stress? Social stress? Performance stress?" Then grab the right tool. And handle it like the capable, resilient human you are. Because stress doesn't have to steal your happiness. Not anymore.

# Chapter 12 Helping Others Reframe: Why You Can't Save People Who Don't Want to Be Saved (And What to Do Instead)

I tried to help my brother for five years.

He was stuck. Not in a crisis—just stuck. Dead-end job he hated. Relationship that was slowly suffocating him. Financial problems that kept getting worse. And every time we talked, it was the same conversation.

"I hate my job." "So quit." "I can't, I need the money." "Then find a better job." "I've tried, nothing ever works out." "Have you updated your resume?" "No, what's the point?"

Round and round. Same circle. Different day.

I'd try to reframe it for him. "What if this job is just a stepping stone? What if you're learning skills you'll need later?" He'd nod. Agree. Say I was right. And then do absolutely nothing.

I'd offer practical help. "Let me look at your resume. Let me connect you with people in my network. Let me help you make a plan." He'd say yes. We'd schedule time. He'd cancel. Reschedule. Cancel again.

After five years of this, I finally asked him: "Do you actually want things to change, or do you just want to complain about them?"

He got defensive. Told me I didn't understand his situation. Said I was being judgmental. That I had it easier than him.

And that's when I realized: He didn't want help. He wanted validation that his situation was hopeless.

Because if his situation was hopeless, he didn't have to do anything about it. He could stay stuck and blame circumstances instead of admitting he was choosing to stay stuck.

That conversation ended badly. We didn't talk for six months. And when we finally did, nothing had changed. He was still stuck. Still complaining. Still blaming.

I'd spent five years trying to help someone who didn't want to be helped.

That was my failure. And it taught me everything I needed to know about helping other people reframe.

* * *

The Hard Truth About Helping People

Here's what nobody tells you when you start learning about reframing, growth mindset, resilience, or any other personal development concept:

Most people don't want to change.

They say they want to change. They complain about their situations. They ask for advice. They nod along when you give it to them.

But they don't actually want to do the work required to change. Because change is uncomfortable. Change requires admitting you've been wrong. Change means giving up familiar suffering for unfamiliar uncertainty.

And for a lot of people, that trade-off isn't worth it.

So they stay stuck. And they surround themselves with people who will validate their stuckness. And they get angry at anyone who suggests they could do something different.

This is the first lesson of helping others: You cannot help someone who doesn't want to be helped.

You can offer tools. You can share frameworks. You can model a different way of thinking. But you cannot force someone to use what you're offering.

And if you try—if you keep pushing, keep offering, keep trying to save them—you'll just exhaust yourself while they stay exactly where they are.

I learned this with my brother. And it took me five years to learn it, which is five years too long.

* * *

The Time It Actually Worked (And Why)

Now let me tell you about someone I did help. We'll call her Rachel.

Rachel was a colleague—someone I worked with on a few projects. She was competent, smart, but perpetually stressed. Every project felt like a crisis to her. Every setback felt like the end of the world.

One day after a meeting where she'd spiraled about a minor client issue, she pulled me aside.

"How do you do it?"

"Do what?"

"Not freak out. I watched you in that meeting. The client was being unreasonable, and you just... handled it. I would have been panicking. How do you stay so calm?"

And here's the difference between Rachel and my brother: Rachel asked for help. Specifically. Genuinely.

She wasn't looking for validation that the situation was hopeless. She was looking for tools to handle it differently.

So I told her about the Dichotomy of Control. List One (things you can't control) versus List Two (things you can).

She didn't just nod along. She pulled out her phone right there and made the lists.

"I can't control whether the client is being reasonable. I can't control the timeline they're demanding. I can't control that they keep changing requirements."

"Okay, List One. Now what can you control?"

"I can control how I communicate the challenges. I can control setting boundaries about what's realistic. I can control asking for help from the team. I can control whether I let this ruin my entire week."

And then she did something crucial: she actually used it.

The next time we had a stressful client situation, she didn't spiral. She made her two lists. She focused on List Two. She handled it.

A few weeks later, she came back with a question: "Okay, the List One/List Two thing works for immediate problems. But how do I stop catastrophizing about things that haven't even happened yet?"

So, I taught her about the Three Paths from Chapter 3—Reaction, Resignation, and Reframing—and the pattern-breaking technique. She implemented those too.

Over the course of about six months, Rachel went from being the person who panicked about everything to being one of the most level-headed people on the team. Not because I fixed her—because she was ready to fix herself and just needed the tools.

That's what successful help looks like. Not you rescuing someone. Someone asking for specific tools and then actually using them.

* * *

How to Tell If Someone Actually Wants Help (Before You Waste Five Years)

After my brother and Rachel, I developed a test. A way to quickly figure out if someone actually wants help or just wants to complain.

Here's how it works:

Step One: Listen to them describe the problem.

Don't interrupt. Don't try to fix it yet. Just listen. Let them get it all out.

Step Two: Ask one simple question: "What have you already tried?"

This is the filter. This is how you know.

If they've tried things—even if those things didn't work—they're ready for help. They're taking action. They're just missing the right approach.

If they haven't tried anything? If their answer is "Nothing works" or "What's the point?" or "It's not that simple"? They're not ready.

Step Three: Offer one specific tool. Not advice—a tool.

Don't say "You should try to be more positive." That's not a tool. That's a platitude.

Say "Here's something that helped me: when I'm spiraling, I make two lists—things I can control and things I can't. Want to try it?"

If they say yes and actually do it, keep going. If they say yes and don't do it, stop offering.

Step Four: Watch what they do, not what they say.

People who want help take action. Even small action. Even imperfect action. They try the tool. They come back with questions. They report what worked and what didn't.

People who don't want help talk about taking action. They say they'll try it. They agree it sounds good. And then nothing changes.

If you see action—even messy, imperfect action—invest your energy there. If you see only talk, walk away.

* * *

What to Do With the People Who Won't Help Themselves

Okay, so you've identified someone who doesn't actually want help. Now what?

If it's a stranger or casual acquaintance, the answer is simple: stop offering. Let them complain. Nod sympathetically. Don't invest energy trying to fix them.

But what if it's someone you care about? Family. Close friend. Romantic partner.

This is harder. Because you want to help. You can see exactly what they need to do. You know the tools that would work. And watching them stay stuck is painful.

But here's what I learned with my brother: Helping someone who doesn't want help doesn't help them. It just hurts you.

So you set boundaries. Not to punish them—to protect yourself.

With my brother, the boundary looked like this:

"I love you. I want you to be happy. But I can't keep having the same conversation where you tell me about your problems and then don't take any action when I offer solutions. So going forward, I'm happy to talk about other things—sports, family, whatever. But I'm not going to keep trying to fix situations you're not willing to work on."

He didn't like it. Told me I was being cold. Unsupportive. A bad brother.

But I held the boundary. And you know what happened?

Nothing. He stayed stuck. But I stopped being exhausted. I stopped feeling guilty that I couldn't save him. I stopped wasting emotional energy on someone who wasn't ready to change.

And weirdly, our relationship got better. Not because he changed—because I stopped trying to force him to change.

That's what boundaries do. They protect your energy so you can invest it in people who are actually ready to receive help.

* * *

How to Actually Help Someone Who's Ready (The Right Way)

Okay, so you've found someone who actually wants help. Someone like Rachel. What now?

Here's what worked:

Give them one tool at a time.

Don't dump your entire personal development library on them. Don't recommend five books and three podcasts and this great TED talk you saw. That's overwhelming.

Give them one specific, actionable tool. "When you're stressed about something, make two lists—what you can control and what you can't." That's it. Let them use it. Let them come back when they're ready for more.

Let them struggle.

This is the hardest part. You want to rescue them. You want to do it for them. You want to protect them from making mistakes.

Don't. Let them try the tool. Let them mess it up. Let them figure out how to apply it to their specific situation.

Rachel didn't use the Dichotomy of Control perfectly at first. She put things in the wrong lists. She still catastrophized sometimes. But she learned by doing it, not by me doing it for her.

Celebrate their effort, not their results.

When Rachel came back and said "I tried the two lists thing and it kind of helped," I didn't critique how she used it. I celebrated that she used it at all.

"That's great. You actually tried it. Most people don't even do that."

People who are learning need reinforcement for trying, not judgment for imperfect execution.

Know when to step back.

After about six months, Rachel didn't need me anymore. She had internalized the tools. She was applying them on her own. She'd figured out how to adapt them to her specific situations.

That's success. Not her becoming dependent on you for answers—her becoming independent and capable.

If you've done it right, they won't need you anymore. And that's exactly what you want.

So here's what I learned from five years of failure with my brother and six months of success with Rachel:

You cannot save people who don't want to be saved.

You can offer tools. You can model a different way of thinking. You can be available when they're ready.

But you cannot force someone to change. And trying to force it will just destroy you both.

So test whether they're ready. Give one tool at a time. Let them struggle. Celebrate effort.

And if they're not ready? Set boundaries and walk away. Not because you don't care—because caring without boundaries is just self-destruction with good intentions.

Save your energy for the people who are ready to receive it.

Because those people exist. And they're worth finding.

# Chapter 13 Your Mind Is Your Home: The Only Space You Actually Control (And How to Stop Letting Squatters Live There)

I used to let people live rent-free in my head.

Not metaphorically. Well, metaphorically. But it felt real.

There was this guy—we'll call him Derek—who worked in my department about twelve years ago. Derek was one of those people who's professionally unpleasant. Not openly hostile, just constantly undermining. He'd shoot down ideas in meetings. Make passive-aggressive comments about other people's work. Take credit for things he didn't do.

And I let him take up residence in my brain.

I'd replay conversations with him while driving home. I'd imagine better comebacks to things he'd said three days ago. I'd rehearse future interactions, scripting exactly what I'd say if he pulled his bullshit again. I'd lie in bed at night composing emails I'd never send.

Derek was living in my head. Not paying rent. Not contributing anything useful. Just taking up space and making the place miserable.

And here's the worst part: Derek didn't even know. He wasn't thinking about me at all. He'd go home and forget I existed. Meanwhile, I was giving him hours of free real estate in my consciousness.

One day, Izzy asked me what I was thinking about. I'd been quiet for twenty minutes, staring out the window while we were supposed to be watching a movie.

"Derek."

"The guy from work? What about him?"

"Just... replaying this thing he said in a meeting."

"When was the meeting?"

"Tuesday."

It was Friday.

She looked at me like I'd lost my mind. "You're spending your Friday night thinking about something Derek said on Tuesday?"

And when she said it out loud, I realized how absurd it was.

I was sitting on the couch with my wife, supposedly watching a movie, but actually giving Derek—someone I didn't even like—my attention, my mental energy, my peace.

That was the moment I understood: your mind is the only space you actually control, and most people are letting it be occupied by squatters.

* * *

Who's Living in Your Head Without Permission?

Think about your own mental space right now. Who's in there?

Not the people you're actively thinking about—the squatters. The people who show up uninvited and won't leave.

Maybe it's a coworker who annoyed you. Maybe it's a family member who criticized you. Maybe it's someone from high school who made you feel small twenty years ago and you're still carrying around that moment.

Maybe it's not even a person—maybe it's a mistake you made, a failure you can't let go of, an embarrassing moment you replay on loop.

These are your squatters. And they're taking up space that could be used for literally anything else.

Here's what's insane about squatters: they're only there because you keep inviting them back.

Derek wasn't forcing me to think about him. I was choosing to replay those conversations. I was choosing to imagine future confrontations. I was choosing to give him my mental energy.

And every minute I spent thinking about Derek was a minute I wasn't spending thinking about something that actually mattered.

That's the cost of squatters. Not just that they make your mental space unpleasant—they take up room that could be used for people and things you actually care about.

* * *

How I Evicted Derek (And How You Can Evict Your Squatters)

After Izzy called me out, I decided Derek needed to go. Not from the company—I couldn't control that. From my head.

But evicting a mental squatter isn't as simple as deciding "I won't think about this anymore." That doesn't work. Try it right now: don't think about a pink elephant. See? You just thought about a pink elephant.

You can't evict a squatter by ignoring them. You have to actively replace them with something else.

Here's what I did:

Step One: I noticed when Derek showed up.

I couldn't stop him from appearing in my thoughts. But I could notice when it happened. I'd catch myself replaying a conversation and think: "Oh, there's Derek again. Uninvited. Not paying rent."

Just noticing was the first step. Not judging myself for it. Not trying to force him out. Just acknowledging: this is happening right now.

Step Two: I asked myself one question: "Is this useful?"

Not "Is this pleasant?" Not "Do I want to think about this?" But "Is thinking about Derek right now actually useful?"

The answer was always no. Replaying past conversations wasn't changing them. Imagining future confrontations wasn't preparing me for anything real. It was just mental rumination disguised as problem-solving.

Step Three: I deliberately redirected my attention.

This is the key. You can't just evict the squatter—you have to move someone else in.

So when I caught myself thinking about Derek, I'd deliberately shift to something that actually mattered. Sometimes it was thinking about a project I was working on. Sometimes it was thinking about plans with Izzy. Sometimes it was just noticing what was actually happening in the present moment—the feel of the steering wheel, the sound of the music, the taste of coffee.

At first, Derek would come right back. I'd redirect, and thirty seconds later he'd be there again. But I kept redirecting. Over and over. Like training a puppy not to jump on furniture.

And after a few weeks, something shifted. Derek started showing up less. And when he did show up, I could redirect faster.

Eventually, he mostly stopped showing up at all. Not because I'd forced him out—because I'd stopped giving him space.

* * *

## It's Not Just People—It's Mental Clutter

Squatters aren't always people. Sometimes they're just mental clutter—thoughts, worries, regrets, what-ifs that take up space without serving any purpose.

I have a friend who spends hours every week mentally redesigning her house. She doesn't have the money to actually renovate. She's not taking any steps toward renovation. She's just... thinking about it. Imagining different paint colors. Rearranging furniture in her mind. Scrolling through Pinterest for ideas she'll never implement.

That's mental clutter. It's not harmful, necessarily. But it's taking up space that could be used for something that actually moves her life forward.

I used to do the same thing with hypothetical arguments. I'd spend mental energy preparing for conversations that would never happen. Defending myself against criticisms nobody had made. Winning imaginary debates with people who didn't even know we were arguing.

All of that was clutter. Useless thoughts taking up valuable mental real estate.

Here's how you know if something in your head is clutter:

Ask yourself: "If I spent this mental energy on something else, would my life be better?"

If the answer is yes, it's clutter. And clutter needs to go.

* * *

Who Actually Gets to Live in Your Mental Space?

Okay, so you've evicted the squatters and cleared out the clutter. Now what?

Now you get to be intentional about what you let in.

Your mental space is finite. You only have so much attention, so much energy, so much capacity to think about things. Every minute you spend thinking about something is a minute you're not spending thinking about something else.

So you get to choose. Who and what deserves that space?

For me, the answer became clear after I evicted Derek:

People I love get space. Thinking about Izzy, planning things with her, being present when we're together—that's worth my mental energy.

Work that matters gets space. Projects I care about, problems I'm actually solving, skills I'm building—that's worth thinking about.

The present moment gets space. What I'm actually experiencing right now—the taste of food, the feeling of sun, the sound of music—that's worth noticing.

Plans and problems I can actually do something about get space. If thinking about something leads to action, it's worth the mental energy.

Everything else? Everything that's just rumination, catastrophizing, replaying the past, imagining arguments that won't happen, worrying about things I can't control?

That doesn't get space. Not because I'm suppressing it—because I'm choosing to use my limited mental real estate for things that actually matter.

* * *

The Daily Mental Housekeeping Practice

Here's what I do now, every single day, to keep my mental space clean:

Morning: Set the intention.

Before I get out of bed, I decide what deserves my mental energy today. Not a to-do list—an attention budget. What people, projects, and problems get space in my head today?

Some days it's: Izzy, the training I'm delivering, and staying present. That's it. Everything else is a squatter.

Throughout the day: Notice and redirect.

When I catch myself thinking about something that's not on my attention budget—when a squatter shows up—I notice it and redirect.

"Oh, there's that worry about money again. Not on today's budget. What actually needs my attention right now?"

I don't judge myself for the squatter showing up. I just redirect. Over and over, all day, as many times as necessary.

Evening: Review and release.

Before bed, I do a quick mental inventory. What occupied my mind today? Was it worth the space it took up?

If I spent too much time on squatters or clutter, I make a note of what triggered it. Not to beat myself up—to catch it earlier tomorrow.

And then I deliberately release whatever doesn't need to come with me into sleep. "That argument I replayed four times? Not bringing that to bed. That worry about next week? Can't do anything about it tonight, so it doesn't get space."

This isn't perfect. I still let squatters in sometimes. I still waste mental energy on clutter. But I catch it faster now. And I'm intentional about what gets to stay.

* * *

## What Changes When You Evict the Squatters

It's been years since I evicted Derek. And here's what's different:

I'm more present. Because I'm not constantly replaying the past or rehearsing the future.

I'm less anxious. Because I'm not giving mental space to things I can't control.

I'm more effective. Because all my problem-solving energy goes to problems I can actually solve.

I'm happier. Not because my circumstances are better—because I'm not wasting mental energy on things that make me miserable.

And most importantly: I'm available. Available to notice good moments. Available to connect with people I care about. Available to actually experience my life instead of living in my head.

That's what happens when you treat your mind like your home. You get to decide who lives there. You get to evict the squatters. You get to clear out the clutter.

And suddenly, you have space for the things that actually matter.

So here's my question for you:

Who's living rent-free in your head right now?

What person, worry, regret, or imaginary scenario is taking up mental real estate that could be used for something that actually matters?

Because your mind is the only space you actually control. Everything else—your circumstances, other people's behavior, external events—that's List One. Can't control it.

But your mental space? That's List Two. That's yours.

So evict the squatters. Clear out the clutter. And make room for what actually deserves to be there.

Because life's too short to spend it thinking about Derek.

# Chapter 14: The Last Thing Standing Between You and Happiness (Spoiler: It's You)

Alright. Here we are. The final pages.

If this were a movie, epic music would swell and you'd walk out of the theater feeling like you could conquer the world. But this isn't a movie. This is your actual life.

There's no orchestra. There's no slow-motion hero walk into the sunset. There's no explosion happening conveniently in the background. There's just you, sitting wherever you're sitting right now, facing a choice that will determine whether the last several hours of reading meant anything—or whether this becomes another book gathering dust on your shelf of good intentions.

So let me be direct with you one last time:

Everything you need to be happy? You already have it. You've had it this whole time. You didn't need this book to give you some magical secret that was hiding from you. You didn't need me to hand you a golden key to a hidden door. All I did—all any of this did—

was hold up a mirror and show you what was getting in the way.

Your brain was the problem. Your perspective was the prison. Your habits of thought were the chains.

And now? Now you know how to break all of it. The only question that matters: Will you?

**The Happiness Algorithm: Your Complete System**

Before the big finish, let's lock in what you've learned. Because your brain is already trying to forget half of it. Here's the complete system:

**Step 1: Catch the Spiral**

Your brain will lie to you. Constantly. It will catastrophize, turn minor inconveniences into existential crises, and convince you everything is worse than it actually is.

Your job? Catch it in the act. The moment that doom-and-gloom narrative starts playing—the moment you feel yourself spiraling—you interrupt it. You don't let it run its program. You stop it cold and say, *"I see what you're doing. Not today."*

**Step 2: Reframe the Situation**

Once you've caught the spiral, flip it. Take the same facts and tell a different story.

- "This is a disaster" becomes "This is a challenge I can handle."
- "Why does this always happen to me?" becomes "What can I learn from this?"

- "Everything is ruined" becomes "What's actually true here?"

Find the "At Least." Shrink the problem to its actual size. Ask what Future You—calm, wise, looking back—would say about this moment.

**Step 3: Choose Your Response**

You have three paths in any difficult situation:

1. Path One: Reaction — React emotionally, make everything worse
2. Path Two: Resignation — Give up, play victim, stay stuck forever
3. Path Three: Reframing — Take control, find the angle, move forward stronger

Path 3. Always Path 3. Even when it's hard. Especially when it's hard.

**Step 4: Protect Your Inputs**

Your brain absorbs whatever you feed it. Garbage in, garbage out. Guard your mental diet. Limit exposure to negativity. Curate your environment. Choose relationships that lift you instead of drain you dry.

**Step 5: Practice Until It's Automatic**

Happiness isn't a one-time decision. It's a daily practice. A muscle built through repetition.

Keep catching spirals. Keep reframing. Keep choosing Path 3. Eventually, it stops being something you think about—it becomes who you are.

That's the algorithm. Simple to understand. Challenging to master. Life-changing when you commit.

**Two Versions of Your Future**

Let me paint you two pictures. Two possible futures. Both equally available to you right now.

**Future #1: You Do Nothing**

You finish this book. You think, *"That was really interesting. I should do that stuff."*

You set it down, check your phone, and within minutes you're absorbed back into your regular life. Within 48 hours, you've forgotten 90% of what you read. Within a week, this book is a vague memory of something that seemed helpful.

Next time stress hits—and it will, probably tomorrow—you react the same way you always have. The familiar spiral. The catastrophic thinking. The same emotional patterns that have been running the show for years.

Months pass. Years pass. And one day you're sitting somewhere, stressed and unhappy, and you vaguely remember reading a book about happiness once. You can't remember what it said. You can't remember the techniques. You just remember it sounded good at the time.

You meant to apply it. You really did. But you didn't.

**Future #2: You Actually Apply This**

You finish this book and think, *"This is the last time I let my brain run the show unchallenged."*

You don't just set it down and move on. You do something. Today. Before the inspiration fades.

Tomorrow morning, you wake up and consciously decide: *"I'm choosing how I feel today. Not my circumstances. Not other people. Me."*

When stress hits that same week, something different happens. You catch the spiral. You recognize the pattern. You think, *"There's my brain being dramatic again."* And instead of believing it, you reframe it. You handle it like the capable human you've always been capable of being.

It feels weird at first. Awkward. Like you're pretending.

But you keep doing it. Day after day. And then one day—maybe a month in, maybe three—you realize something has fundamentally shifted. You're calmer. More resilient. More at peace. Not because life got easier—but because you got better at living it.

People start noticing. They ask what changed. And you smile because it wasn't one big thing. It was a thousand small choices to think differently, react differently, show up differently.

Two futures. Same person standing at the crossroads. The only difference is what you do next.

**Why Most People Stay Stuck**

Here's something I saved for the end:

Most people who read self-help books don't change. I know that's a weird thing for an author to admit. But it's true, and you need to hear it.

Not because the books are bad. Not because the advice doesn't work. Because the readers never implement anything. They read, highlight, feel inspired for 72 hours. Maybe they tell a friend about it. Maybe they post about it online.

Then they slide right back into their old patterns like nothing happened. Why? Because change is uncomfortable. And your brain hates discomfort more than it hates being unhappy.

Think about that. Your brain would rather keep you stuck in familiar misery than push you into unfamiliar growth. It would rather you stay exactly who you've always been—even if who you've always been isn't working.

So when you try to think differently, your brain resists. It says, *"This is weird. This isn't us."*

When you try to reframe, it says, *"This is stupid. The problem is still real."*

When you try to choose happiness, it says, *"But what about all these legitimate things to worry about?"*

If you listen to that voice? If you obey the resistance? You lose. You go right back to being who you were before page one.

The people who actually change their lives push through the discomfort anyway. They practice the techniques even when their brain says it won't work. They show up differently even when every old habit screams at them to go back to normal.

That's the price of transformation. Temporary discomfort for permanent change. Are you willing to pay it?

**Your 7-Day Initiation**

I'm not letting you close this book without a concrete challenge. Because I've seen the statistics, and I know human nature. If you don't act within the next seven days, you probably never will.

The inspiration fades. The motivation evaporates. Life gets busy. And before you know it, this book is just another thing you read once.

So, here's your initiation into your new life. Seven days. Seven challenges. No excuses.

**Day 1: The Morning Decision**

Before your feet hit the floor, before you check your phone—decide out loud: *"I choose how I feel today. Not my circumstances. Me."*

**Day 2: Catch Three Spirals**

Just notice when your brain is catastrophizing. Don't fix it yet. Just catch it three times and acknowledge: *"There's my brain being dramatic again."*

**Day 3: Reframe Everything**

Every problem today—big or small—gets reframed. Traffic jam? *"At least I can finish that podcast."* Plans canceled? *"At least I have unexpected free time."* Force it, even when it feels ridiculous. Especially then.

**Day 4: The Input Audit**

Look honestly at what you're feeding your brain—news, social media, people, conversations. Identify ONE source of negativity and eliminate it. Unfollow. Mute. Walk away. Today.

**Day 5: Do Something Uncomfortable**

Have the conversation you've been avoiding. Send the message you've been drafting in your head. Try the thing you've been afraid to fail at. Prove to yourself you can handle discomfort and survive.

**Day 6: Invest in Joy**

Do something that makes you happy. Not productive. Not responsible. Just happy. Call the friend. Take the walk. Watch the thing without guilt. Happiness isn't just removing negatives—it's adding positives.

**Day 7: Burn the Old You**

Write down three beliefs, habits, or patterns that have been holding you back. The stories you tell yourself. The excuses you make. Then destroy that paper—burn it, tear it up, throw it away with intention.

That version of you? Gone. The new version—the one who controls their mind and refuses to let life steal their peace—that's all that remains.

**The Final Truth**

Here's what I really want you to understand. The thing underneath everything else:

You were never broken. You didn't need to be fixed. You didn't need someone to save you. You didn't need to become a fundamentally different person.

You just needed to see things differently. The same events. The same circumstances. The same problems everyone faces. But viewed through a different lens—a lens you control, that you choose, that you can adjust whenever you want.

That's all happiness ever was. Not the absence of problems. Not perfect circumstances. Not some magical external thing you had to chase and capture.

Just a different way of seeing what's already in front of you. And now that you can see it? You can't unsee it. You can't go back to believing you're powerless over your own mind. You can't go back to thinking happiness is something that happens to you. You can't go back to letting your brain run unchallenged, believing every catastrophic thought like it's gospel truth.

You know too much now. Which means the only question left is whether you'll use what you know—or waste it.

**One Last Thing Before You Go**

You made it. You actually finished. That puts you ahead of most people who start books like this. So genuinely—congratulations. You showed up. You stuck with it.

But finishing the book was never the accomplishment. Living it is.

**So, here's my final charge:**

1. Stop waiting for the right moment. There isn't one. There never was.

2. Stop waiting until you feel ready. You never will. Readiness is a decision, not a feeling.
3. Stop waiting for permission. This is it. I'm giving it to you. Right now.
4. Go be happy. Not because your life is perfect—it's not, and it never will be. Not because everything worked out—some things won't. But because you decided to be. Because you took control of the one thing you could always control—your own mind. Because you refused to let circumstances, other people, or your own brain's drama dictate how you experience your one precious life.

Happiness was never out there somewhere, hiding in your future, waiting for you to find it. It was in here all along—waiting for you to choose it. So choose it. Right now. And every single day after.

Go be happy, dammit. The End.

**(Or, you know... the beginning.)**

# About the Author

**Ken Konet – King of Overthinking, Dodger of Rakes, and Excited Finisher of Books.**

Oh, hey there. You've made it to the "About the Author" section—either because you're genuinely interested in the mastermind behind this literary chaos or because you accidentally flipped too far while doomscrolling through your Kindle. Either way, welcome!

I'm Ken Konet, an *Instructional Designer, IT Engineer, Corporate Trainer, and professional "why am I still awake at 3 AM" thinker.* I have spent the last decade (yes, a whole decade) working on way too many books at the same time—because why finish one when you can juggle twelve? But now, as *retirement creeps closer and my wife kindly (read: aggressively) reminds me that it's time to actually finish these projects*, I'm finally hitting *Publish* on books that have been sitting in my brain (and on my hard drive) for far too long.

**What Have I Actually Managed to Finish?**

Recently, I've unleashed onto the world:

✓ *Move Forward* – a self-improvement book for those who want to ditch procrastination and build momentum (without relying on motivation, because let's be real, it never shows up when you need it).

✓ *Stop Stepping on Rakes* – a humorous, painfully relatable guide to learning from life's mistakes without taking yourself too seriously (because stepping on metaphorical rakes is an art form).

✓ The Engaged Leader – *Ditch outdated leadership nonsense and learn how to actually engage, inspire, and lead without making your team secretly plot your downfall.*

✓ Several novels and a few other books on a wide variety of subjects. These are all projects I've been working on for decades. With all the travel I do for work, I am finally able to spend much needed time finishing these projects for all to enjoy.

**Who is This Guy Anyway?**

I hold two MBAs and a Master's in Education (because clearly, one degree wasn't enough). I've spent my career teaching, writing, and designing learning experiences for humans who want to *figure out life, avoid self-sabotage, and make fewer bad decisions (or at least funnier ones).*

When I'm not *overanalyzing existence*, I'm:

✓ Riding motorcycles with my wife Izzy (*because life is more fun on two wheels*).

✓ Camping and hiking (*getting lost in the woods builds character*).

✓ Tinkering with technology (*someone has to explain why your Wi-Fi sucks*).

✓ Trying to outsmart my ADHD brain (*usually fighting my distractions, but at least it's entertaining*).

If you've made it this far, congrats—you now know more about me than my doctor does. If you enjoy funny, sarcastic, painfully honest self-improvement, stick around. There's more where this came from.

---

**THE END**

www.ingramcontent.com/pod-product-compliance
Lightning Source LLC
LaVergne TN
LVHW030911080826
845145LV00010B/2859

* 9 7 8 1 9 6 6 7 0 3 0 7 5 *